THE VALIDITY OF
THE GOSPEL RECORD

THE INTERNATIONAL LIBRARY OF CHRISTIAN KNOWLEDGE

Edited by

DR. WILLIAM ADAMS BROWN AND DR. BERTRAM LEE WOOLF

JEW AND GREEK: TUTORS UNTO CHRIST

THE JEWISH AND HELLENISTIC BACKGROUND OF THE NEW TESTAMENT

By G. H. C. MACGREGOR, M.A., B.D. (Cantab.), D.Litt. (Glas.),
D.D. (Edin.), and A. C. PURDY, A.B., B.D., Ph.D. (Hartford).

A HISTORY OF RELIGION IN THE OLD TESTAMENT

By MAX LOEHR (*Professor in the University of Koenigsberg*).

A FRESH APPROACH TO THE NEW TESTAMENT AND
EARLY CHRISTIAN LITERATURE

By MARTIN DIBELIUS (*Professor in the University of Heidel-
berg*).

THE BEGINNINGS OF THE CHRISTIAN CHURCH

(Being the first volume of "A History of the Early Church")
By HANS LIETZMANN (*Professor in the University of Berlin*).

THE FOUNDING OF THE CHURCH CATHOLIC

(Being the second volume of "A History of the Early Church")
By HANS LIETZMANN (*Professor in the University of Berlin*).

THE PHILOSOPHY OF RELIGION

FROM THE STANDPOINT OF PROTESTANT THEOLOGY

By EMIL BRUNNER (*Professor in the University of Zürich*).

A FRESH APPROACH TO THE PSALMS

By W. O. E. OESTERLEY, D.D., Litt.D. (*Professor of Hebrew
and Old Testament Exegesis at King's College, University of
London*).

THE VALIDITY OF THE GOSPEL RECORD

By ERNEST FINDLAY SCOTT, D.D. (*Professor of New Testament
Criticism, Union Theological Seminary, New York*).

THE VALIDITY OF
THE GOSPEL RECORD

By

ERNEST FINDLAY SCOTT, D.D.

Professor of New Testament Criticism
Union Theological Seminary
New York

NEW YORK
CHARLES SCRIBNER'S SONS
1938

59-15 39

PREFACE

FOR a long time past the Christian mind has been steadily turning from doctrines about Christ to the historical facts. It would be easy to enumerate at least fifty books, written within the last few years, in which the life of Jesus has been presented from every conceivable point of view. They all bear witness to the growing conviction that before we can understand the religion of Jesus we must know more of him as an historical Person. This interest in the life has led to an ever more searching enquiry into the documents which record it. Some of the acutest minds of our time have been engaged in this investigation, and not a year passes but some new and unexpected light is thrown on the familiar Gospels.

This intensive study, to which we owe so much, has in some ways confused the issues. A picture loses its outlines when it is examined close at hand through a magnifying glass. The Gospel history, under critical scrutiny, tends to dissolve into a mass of unmeaning fragments. An impression has been created that the evidence of the records has broken down, and that the truth about Jesus, if he ever lived at all, has now vanished beyond recovery.

The aim of the present book is to call attention to some factors which have too often been overlooked in the consideration of the Gospel testimony. It is now admitted that our existing Gospels have grown out of an earlier tradition, which was handed down orally before it was committed to writing. The credibility of the record depends on the value of that tradition; and the author has sought to discover how it was formed and transmitted. He acknowledges his debt to the many eminent scholars who have worked on this problem, but who have sometimes failed, in his opinion, to perceive the true significance of their own findings.

He is himself convinced, as he has tried to show in the following chapters, that the Gospels have every claim to be accepted as substantially a record of fact. Their evidence would hardly be challenged if they were concerned with some other hero of antiquity, and it is only because they recount the life of Jesus that they are viewed suspiciously. This is not unreasonable, for since our religion is bound up with the validity of these Gospels no criticism that we apply to them can be too exacting. Yet they ought to be treated with the same fairness as other historical documents. If they can be proved, by all the customary tests, to embody a sound tradition, they ought not to be discounted on any purely arbitrary grounds. The present book will have served its purpose if it helps to secure this justice for the Gospel records.

E. F. SCOTT

CONTENTS

THE VALIDITY OF
THE GOSPEL RECORD

CHAPTER I

THE GOSPELS AS HISTORY

Our records of the life of Jesus have all come to us from a later age. The oldest Gospel, that of Mark, may have been written about 70 A.D., and the two longer Gospels of Matthew and Luke nearly twenty years afterwards. Can there be much historical value in these belated records? They belong to a time when the immediate followers of Jesus had passed from the scene, and a haze of legend had settled on his memory. They were drawn up by men who were steeped in theological ideas, and could no longer distinguish the doctrines from the facts. What is given us in the Gospels is not so much an authentic record as the myth which the church had woven, out of a few uncertain traditions, around the life of its Founder.

This conclusion, to which criticism seemed to be driven a century ago, has now been largely corrected by criticism. It has been demonstrated that although the Gospels themselves are late, they have been compiled from earlier documents, and these from still earlier ones. In recent years the effort has been made to get behind all documents. It may be taken as certain that the Christian message was first proclaimed, and for a considerable time was handed down by word of mouth. While men were still living who had known Jesus personally they could speak of him at first hand, and such teaching was far more welcome and effective than any which might be conveyed through books. It was believed, too, that the Lord would return at any moment to bring in the Kingdom, and there could be no purpose in writing down a record of him for a future age which would never come.

At the outset, therefore, all Christian instruction was by word of mouth, and it is here we encounter the baffling factor in the investigation of the history. With written documents we are on firm ground. The facts are set down in black and white, and all later departures from them can be brought to the test. When a written statement is known to exist there is, indeed, little temptation to devise fanciful stories which can at once be exposed. As soon as it was put into writing the Gospel history was fixed. Apocryphal tales of Jesus grew up abundantly in the second century, but no one took them seriously, since they could be checked by the Gospels. Within the Gospels themselves the modern critic seeks to determine the sections which were written earliest, for here he has the standard by which he can judge the value of all later additions. The very purpose of writing is to guard the known facts from those perversions which are sure to creep in when everything is left to the spoken word. In so far, then, as our Gospels are based on written sources they may be deemed trustworthy, but it has always to be borne in mind that these sources contained the facts only as they were reported at the time of writing. There is no reason to doubt that the writers put down honestly what they knew; but what did they know? Only those memories of Jesus which had undergone all the wear and tear of a period of oral tradition. How long that period had lasted we cannot tell. Some of the written documents may go back to a date as early as twenty years after Jesus' death, or even earlier. But they still leave us with an interval of years during which the facts were orally transmitted. Each person who recounted the story of Jesus was free to exercise his own prejudice or fancy, and there was no means of correcting him. Every one knows how an incident becomes distorted when it is left to hearsay for even a few weeks or days. Is there any reason to believe that the events of Jesus' life fared any better, as they passed from one narrator to another in those early days of the church? That period of oral transmission, however short we may contrive to make it, must always be the chief obstacle to our knowledge of the life of Jesus. It may be granted that our evangelists, and the authors of their sources, faithfully put down the record which had come to them; but what had happened to the record in the preceding years? Under what conditions had it been transmitted? Had any precautions been taken to secure it against the many accidents which waylaid it as it passed from mouth to mouth?

One fact has emerged clearly from the modern investigation. It has been established that the Gospels assumed their present form gradually, as enlargements or revisions of previous works which had served the same purpose in a less adequate manner. When Mark wrote his Gospel he would not think of himself as doing something which was entirely new. He was merely continuing, with a little more skill and knowledge, the work of teachers before him. His aim was to follow their methods as far as possible, and to incorporate what they had given him. This is how the two later evangelists have dealt with Mark, and we may infer that he had done the same with his predecessors.[1] It may likewise be inferred that those earlier writers were in the same position as Mark. They also were not attempting anything new. They collected and arranged the material which had come to them, in the manner approved by previous teachers. To be sure they put into writing what had hitherto been delivered orally, and this was an innovation. Yet it did not affect the content of their record, or even its form, but was only a mechanical device for assisting the memory. There was thus a direct continuity between the later tradition and the earlier. In a real sense the Gospels as we have them provide the clue to what the record had always been. They were not works of a new character, based, to some extent, on the primitive reminiscences. They contain the primitive record itself, as it had been preserved and transmitted by a succession of teachers.

In the study of all documents, and particularly of the Gospels, we need to be on constant guard against what

[1]*Cf.* B. H. Branscomb (*Commentary on the Gospel of Mark*, xxii f.); gives an excellent summary of the arguments.

may be called the literary illusion. As they pass from the spoken to the written form words seem to acquire a new quality. Something is said in ordinary conversation, and you hardly listen to it. When you see it in print, although it is still the same foolish or trivial statement, you feel, in spite of yourself, that it is important. The power of the press is founded on this weakness in human nature, to which no one is so liable as the professional critic. He takes for granted that all writings must be treated with reverence. He dates a nation's literature from its first book—usually a dull chronicle which is not to be compared with the tales and ballads current among the people. So in Biblical criticism the authors of written documents are placed, as a matter of course, in a higher class by themselves. The history of Hebrew prophecy is divided sharply into two periods—that in which the prophets merely spoke their oracles and presumably had little to say, and the true age of the writing prophets. The early history of the church is likewise divided into the period before Paul, when nothing was written, and the period of real activity which opened with Paul's Epistles. Yet it is evident, on a little reflection, that the mere act of writing made no intrinsic difference. Elijah and Elisha were prophets, in the same sense as Amos and Hosea. Paul never conceived of himself as called to a different work from Peter because he happened sometimes to write down what he was prevented from speaking. The written word is permanent, and it makes all the difference to us now that the thoughts of some men have been preserved, while those of others have gone with the breath that uttered them. Yet the writing is only speech in another form, and in no way changes the nature of the message.

This must always be borne in mind when we consider the Gospels in their relation to the earlier tradition. Mark gave fixity to the church's records by compiling them in a book, but he was not for that reason an innovator. He merely transferred to paper what the other teachers had passed on by word of mouth. He recorded the same facts as they did, with the same purpose, and in much the same words. For that part, he was one in a succession of teachers who had already made use of writing. With various objects in view they had thrown into this form some of the things which they were accustomed to speak, and were not aware that by so doing they had made any real change.

So between the Gospels and the previous tradition there was a vital continuity. It is commonly said that the process which led up to the making of our Gospels is shrouded in darkness, but this is not strictly true. Although we know nothing of the earlier teachers we can tell how they dealt with the tradition, for they were in a direct line with our evangelists, and went about their work in the same manner. "Oral tradition" and "written documents" appear at first sight to be different things, and criticism has made great play with the supposed difference. But the documents are nothing essentially but the tradition put into writing. No doubt the act of writing entailed more conciseness of language and a more studied arrangement; but in its substance the record was the same. This, indeed, was necessary if the new Gospels were to win acceptance. The Christian public had to feel assured that nothing had been changed in the teaching through the different method of presentation. Here in a book was the familiar record which had been known hitherto in oral form. One might compare the evangelists with those mediæval builders who replaced the old wooden churches with structures of stone. The material was different, and made possible a new and more elaborate architecture; but the churches conformed to the same general plan as the old ones, and were adapted to the same type of worship. There was no feeling of strangeness in passing from the old buildings to the new.

From our present Gospels, therefore, we may infer the nature of the earlier records, and the interests by which the church was guided in collecting and preserving them. No definite line can be drawn between the Gospels as we have them and the tradition out of which they grew. This is a conclusion which can hardly be pressed too strongly, since it is completely overlooked in much of the modern criticism. We are given to understand that at a certain point the church conceived the idea of making a history of Jesus out of the vague reminiscences which had come down to it. A number of anecdotes were current which had hitherto been prized, when they were known at all, for the sake of their edifying moral. These were now taken seriously. They were held to embody the facts of Jesus' life, and were placed in sequence, and were fitted into some kind of biographical framework. It is maintained that in any attempt to recover the truth about Jesus this artifice of the evangelists must be disregarded. They have imposed on their material a coherence and an historical quality which it did not possess, and the work of the investigator is to break up the Gospels into their elements, and to seek in these for some possible grains of fact. No record of Jesus can be pieced together, since it never existed; but a few things reported about him in the generation following his death may be sifted out from the later legend, and in this way we may obtain at least a glimpse of the historical figure.[2] This method of enquiry, although at first sight it may appear severely scientific, is based on an assumption for which there is no ground whatever. It takes for granted that in our Gospels the tradition made a new beginning, and we know from criticism, if it has taught us anything, that the evangelists took up a work already in process. They adhered closely to the earlier documents, and these, in turn, were linked with an oral tradition. So far from concealing or misrepresenting the primitive account of Jesus, our Gospels afford us the one safe clue to its nature. In order to penetrate the dark period before the Gospels, we have to examine the aim and character of the Gospels themselves.

There is nothing in literature that exactly corresponds with those Gospels. Attempts have been made to find parallels to them in the sacred books of various

[2]The theory is pushed to its limit in C. A. H. Guignebert, *Jésus.*

religions, or in biographical writings of ancient or mediæval times, but all comparisons break down at some
crucial point. It is evident that the Gospels were not
written according to any stated pattern, but grew, in a
manner of their own, out of conditions which were in
many ways unique. They differ from each other in
plan and outlook, but in all of them three main interests are interwoven. This is at once apparent in the
Gospels of Matthew, Mark and Luke, and hardly less
so in the Fourth Gospel, although it must be placed
in a different category from the other three. (1) In
the first place they are written in the interest of a given
message. Jesus was proclaimed by the church as the
Messiah, through whom God had offered salvation to
his people, and it is shown in the Gospels how he had
fulfilled the Messianic prophecies, how his work had
been accompanied with a divine power, how his teaching
had borne witness to an immediate knowledge of God's
will, how his death was the supreme act, divinely ordained, by which the Kingdom of God was to be realised. The Gospels have manifestly been written under
the influence of this belief in Jesus. Their selection of
sayings and incidents has been determined by it; and
to this extent their purpose is a theological, or, it would
be more just to say, a religious one.

(2) Again, they were intended for the practical guidance of the Christian brotherhood. Matthew and Luke
have incorporated with their narrative a full collection
of Jesus' sayings on man's duty to God and to his fel-
low-men, on work for the Kingdom, on the inward

disposition that belongs to the true servant of God. In Mark also the main outline of the teaching is clearly indicated, and the actions of Jesus are so described as to give an example to his followers. The church as an institution had grown up in the time subsequent to Jesus, and no counsel could be offered to it directly in words that purported to be his own. But it is not difficult to see, as we read between the lines of any of these Gospels, that the church is constantly in the writer's mind. In the light of Jesus' own teaching the Christian community is advised as to how it should order its fellowship and deal with its various problems. Christianity was not only a form of belief but a mode of living which had to be practised within the bonds of a society, and one of the main purposes of the Gospels is to make clear to Christians the nature of the life to which they were committed. Each of the writings, considered in one of its aspects, is a hand-book for the practical guidance of believers.

(3) The chief interest of the Gospels is historical. They are meant to inspire faith in Jesus and to teach his rule of life; but as the necessary foundation of all else they explain who he was and what he had done and suffered. Luke, in the prelude to his Gospel, expressly declares that his object is to impart this knowledge. Many had undertaken to recount the facts of Jesus' life, on the ground of the testimony offered by his immediate followers: this new work is written to put all the material in order and to present it fully and accurately. There is no reason to doubt that Luke has

here stated the principal aim which he had in view; he may have had other aims—religious, ethical, apologetic —but he was not seeking to further some ulterior object under the pretence of writing a history. His primary concern was with the facts. It was on these that Theophilus and all his other readers wished to be better informed, and he has set himself to answer the demand. This is equally true of the other two evangelists, although they do not state their motive in the same explicit terms. They may have other motives, as Luke himself has, but these are apparent only on close analysis, or require to be read in by ingenious conjecture and inference. The historical motive is written large over every paragraph. Whatever else these writings are they are records of the acts and teachings of Jesus. This is the sense in which their readers have always understood them, and which they were plainly meant to bear.

Since this is the purpose of the Gospels we need not question that it was likewise the purpose of the documents which lay behind them. It cannot be assumed that the church, after long contenting itself with abstract reflection on Jesus, awoke suddenly to the need of knowing something about him, and that the evangelists, aware of this need, laid hold of the few doubtful traditions which were still current, and wove them into the semblance of a history. The Gospels are compiled from documents of the same character as themselves. They merely present in a more adequate form what the church already possessed. Luke testifies in his prelude to the eager interest which had long been felt in the doings of Jesus, and which many writers had sought to satisfy. This interest had existed from the first, and one of the chief tasks of all Christian teachers was to impart the knowledge which had come to them. The evangelists continue this work of instruction.

Admittedly the Gospels are more elaborate than the earlier records, and this was the very reason why they were written. But since they were works of the same order as those which they displaced we can learn something from them as to the nature of the previous tradition. It is evident, for one thing, that they are composed with great care. This is particularly noticeable in the work of Matthew, who must have thought out his plan with almost mathematical precision, and has been hardly less precise in matters of detail. One has only to think of the Sermon on the Mount, in which detached sayings are chosen out from a number of sources and linked together so skilfully that they form a consecutive discourse. Luke's Gospel is composed more freely, but for that reason is still more a work of art. All the episodes appear to follow each other naturally and spontaneously, and yet are so ordered that the story unfolds itself with a true dramatic movement. The Gospel of Mark is cruder in its workmanship, and Papias, in the first criticism ever made of it,[3] objects to its want of "order"—meaning, no doubt, that it is more like a disjointed chronicle than a finished work. Yet the narrative of Mark, for all its apparent bareness, is perhaps more carefully constructed than any of the others. Al-

[3] Quoted in Eusebius, III:39.

though he is wanting in literary skill the author has arranged his material with rare judgment. It is now generally acknowledged that the sequence of events is most intelligible when Mark's order is followed; and this can be due to no mere happy accident. Mark has been at trouble with his work. He has never put down anything until he has decided, to the best of his knowledge, where it ought to stand.

This care displayed in the making of the Gospels is highly significant. It shows, for one thing, that the church valued its records, and expected them to be handled conscientiously. As we compare the Gospels with one another we cannot but be struck with the anxiety to keep close to an approved tradition. In all of them the same verse is often repeated word for word, just as it had been handed down. When a serious change is made it seems usually to be due to the use of an alternative record, which, after due consideration, has been preferred. In not a few instances a saying or incident is recorded twice, because it had been found in two somewhat different versions and neither of them could be put aside. Throughout their work the evangelists are content to act as compilers, and this is certainly not because they were lacking in creative power. Luke, more particularly, had a fervid imagination, which it cost him an effort to restrain, and he could easily have invented, instead of piecing together the data of his sources. The reason why the Gospels are compilations must be sought in reverence for the tradition, which could not be discarded or falsified. It had to be reproduced with all fidelity, and as far as possible in the very words with which the church was familiar. Sometimes the evangelist does not himself understand a saying of Jesus, and yet feels obliged to report it. Sometimes it runs counter to his own conception of Jesus' message, but he does not venture to leave it out. All the writers are conscious of an obligation laid upon them to transmit the record in the form approved by the church.

It must here be repeated that our Gospels were intended to replace previous works, of substantially the same character. Matthew and Luke are enlargements of Mark, which was written perhaps twenty years earlier. Mark itself, there is every reason to believe, had been enlarged in a similar manner from a work already existing. Nothing in Gospel literature appears at first sight to be so original as Matthew's compendium of Jesus' main teaching in the Sermon on the Mount. Hitherto the thought of Jesus had only been known in separate aphorisms. Matthew has hit on this bold device of a continuous discourse in which it may be presented as a whole. Yet it is evident, when we compare this section of Matthew with the sixth chapter of Luke, that a number of the principal sayings had already been grouped together. Not only here but everywhere else our evangelists have availed themselves of the work of previous editors. Wherever there is a cluster of kindred sayings or incidents in one Gospel, we are pretty sure to find it in another; and this is only one of many signs that long before the date of our present Gospels the record had in some degree been sifted and consoli-

dated. It may fairly be said, indeed, that our evangelists fell heirs to two traditions—that of the facts
concerning Jesus and that of the methods by which this
material should be treated.

It was expected, therefore, that certain principles
should be observed in the transmission of the record.
The work was a responsible one, and those entrusted
with it were bound by the example of earlier teachers.
This did not mean that they must only repeat, blindly
and credulously, what had been said before, for it had
always been required that the teacher should use his
judgment. It was his duty to examine the record and
correct it wherever it was deficient. This, it can be
shown, was the manner in which our evangelists have
understood their task. They have taken pains to arrange their material, alike in their general plan and in
matters of detail. When they have several accounts to
choose from they have either tried to blend them or
have decided on one in preference to the others. Their
object is to preserve the record and at the same time
hand it down in an improved form. Does this imply,
however, that they sought to improve it historically?
They, and likewise their predecessors, may have taken the
facts for granted, and devoted their whole effort to
orderly presentation. Or they may have been indiffer-
ent to the facts as such, and sought only to bring out,
more forcibly than had hitherto been done, the religious
truth involved in them. A dramatist may deal admirably with some historical episode and yet trouble himself little with the accuracy of every detail. The Chris-

tian teachers may have taken a similar attitude towards their work. They were bound to do their very best with the tradition, but this did not mean that they were responsible for all the facts. Their task was one of presentation, not of research.

It is often contended that our Gospels make no pretension to serious historical value.[4] Behind them, it may be granted, lie some genuine recollections of the life of Jesus, but these have been overlaid with a mass of legend and doctrine and symbolism. The evangelists are content to take over all the material without any question. They had no conception of what history means and never dreamed of historical method. The Gospels have been assigned to various classes of literature, but the suggestion is rarely made that they may be ranked as history. They are compared to the Lives of the Saints, the Northern Sagas, the Jewish Haggada, the legendary memoirs of Greek thaumaturgists. Yet it cannot be denied that they remind us most obviously of historical writings. That is how men have always read them, and how their authors must have intended them to be read. May there not be some solid ground for this estimate of their character?

They have certainly come to us from a time when the idea of history was by no means unknown. Some of the greatest of all historians had already written, and had established the historical methods which have been followed, in all essentials, to this day. Not only so, but

[4]Drews, Couchod, Kalthoff, W. B. Smith and others would resolve the whole history into myth or allegory. A. F. Loisy (*La naissance du christianisme*) and C. A. H. Guignebert (*Jésus*) allow the very minimum of historical fact.

the first century was, in a pre-eminent degree, an age of history-writing. With the decay of free political life interest had been diverted to the past. With the decline of creative art the literature of the time found its natural channel in works of history. It may be objected that the makers of our Gospels were outside of the literary movement; but fashions in literature, as in everything else, have a strange way of diffusing themselves. Bunyan, it is pretty certain, knew nothing of Spenser and the other allegorical poets, but in an age when allegory was cultivated he found means of putting his thought into that form. It cannot be deemed impossible that in the first century, when literary men from the Emperor Claudius downward were writing history, there were also historians in the Christian church.

If they knew nothing of the classical histories the Christian teachers at least had access to Jewish literature, above all to the Old Testament. The books of Samuel and Kings are in a real sense historical works, and the evangelists have plainly studied them and used them as models. They were doubtless acquainted, too, with such later histories as the books of the Maccabees, and perhaps with similar writings of their own time. There are many evidences that in the first century Jewish authors were peculiarly active in the field of history. Josephus was engaged on his great works in the very years when the Gospels of Matthew and Luke appear to have been written. He acknowledges his debt to authors who had preceded him, and we may fairly speak of a school of Jewish historians which flourished in the period between 50 and 100 A.D. If our Gospels had not been Christian writings they would have taken their place as admirable examples of Jewish historical literature, and there is no just reason for denying their historical character because they deal with the acts of Jesus and not with those of Herod or Annas the high-priest.

Not only did the evangelists write with historical models before them, but they have demonstrably used the methods with which competent historians have always worked. They have gone back to sources. They have weighed various testimonies against each other, and exercised their judgment carefully as to which one should be accepted. When no information has come to them they say nothing—with the result that there are gaps and abrupt transitions in their narrative, which they doubtless regretted as much as we do. There have been popular historians, both in ancient and modern times, who relied for their data on one single document, and filled in all the blanks in their knowledge with general reflections or imaginary pictures. The evangelists have not worked in this facile manner. That brief preface in which Luke tells us what he has sought to do describes almost to the letter the aims and methods of any serious historian in our own time. He has tried, in the light of the early documents, to trace accurately the course of all things from the beginning, so as to produce an orderly and trustworthy narrative. This has equally been the object of Mark and Matthew, whose Gospels correspond so closely with that of Luke; and it is hard to see why writings of this character should be denied the name of history.

It may be argued that these considerations only apply to the Gospels as we now have them—works of trained writers, who collected the early traditions and tried to reproduce them in the form of history. Livy has recounted the stories of Romulus and the legendary kings with the same gravity and circumstance as when he afterwards describes the Punic War. They read like history, but it does not follow that they are so. The art of a skilful historian has thrown the illusion of reality over the data of folk-lore and old songs and liturgies. But this comparison is beside the mark. Our Gospels are not the creation of literary art, working on nothing else but a few popular tales. They are made out of documents which, for the most part, are copied almost word for word. If they bear the appearance of history this is not a quality which has been imposed on them but one which has passed into them from the earlier records. The evangelists write as historians, and this was also true, so far as we can judge, of those who had worked before them on the tradition of Jesus. It seems to have been treated from the first in what may fairly be called an historical spirit. From all that we can learn of it the primitive church was not made up exclusively of simple-minded people, who were prepared to accept anything. In the earliest days, much more than afterwards, freedom was of the very essence of the brotherhood. Its members may have been of one heart, but the book of Acts itself provides evidence that they were hardly of one mind. Disputes arose, almost from the outset, which threw the little group of believers into separate camps. In such a community doubtful statements would not easily pass muster, and evidence would be scrutinized. It must never be forgotten, too, that for many years personal disciples of Jesus were still alive and were held in peculiar honour. Their testimony was always available on matters of historical fact, and we know that it was given. Paul is careful to note, in his account of the Resurrection appearances, that his teaching agreed with that of the Apostles, and we need not doubt that a similar warrant was constantly demanded. All Jews were trained from childhood in the habit of appeal to some binding authority—the text of scripture, the custom of the elders, the word of an outstanding Rabbi. The primary authority for the life and teaching of Jesus was the witness of his disciples; and whatever was questioned in the record would be brought to this touchstone. Here, indeed, we may find the guiding principle by which an approved tradition gradually took shape in the church. Out of all the mass of rumour the Christian teachers sought to determine those things which could be traced back, directly or through accredited testimony, to the original disciples. "As they delivered them unto us who from the beginning were eye-witnesses and ministers of the word." This, according to Luke, was the rule he went by when he examined the varied pieces of information which had come to his hand, and this, we may be reasonably sure, was the test which had always been applied.

It may therefore be maintained that in our Gospels we have the final deposit of a genuine historical tradition. This does not imply that everything contained in them must be accepted as indubitable fact. There can be no serious question that the stream of tradition, flowing on through two generations, had gathered into it many elements which impress the modern reader as plainly unhistorical—miraculous actions and interventions, voices from heaven, angelic appearances, supernatural foresight. In most cases these probably go back to the earliest phase of the record, and had place in the teaching of immediate witnesses. It must always be remembered that the ancient mind worked on assumptions which have now become untenable. The higher world was conceived in realistic fashion, and many things were construed as miracle which we should now explain by natural causes. Looking back on the life of Jesus under the full conviction that he was Messiah, the disciples would see all his action in a supernatural light, and their testimony, given in perfect good faith, would be received without any of the doubting criticism which it now awakens. What surprises us is not that these things find a place in the Gospels but that they are comparatively so few. The narrative, however, might have been just as historical although it had been full of that element which might seem at first sight to discredit it.

We have to do with a history attested by men of the ancient world, whose attitude of mind was different from ours. Their interpretation of the facts does not affect the facts themselves.

It is no longer on the ground of that miraculous element in the Gospels that the modern enquiry is disposed to question their historical value. Allowance is now made for the ancient mode of presentation, but it is maintained that the facts, as such, cannot be reconciled with an actual life of Jesus. Everywhere in the narrative there appear to be traces of ideas and influences which only became operative after his death. A community had come into being which made him the central figure in its worship, and built up a legend to justify the central place it gave him. A theology had shaped itself around his Person, and the later doctrines were read back into the history, and in some measure created it. Difficulties of a practical nature were continually arising in the life of the church, and Jesus was conceived as answering them by some pregnant saying, or by his action in a given situation. It is argued that for the true origin of the tradition we must look to this experience of the later church. On the grounds, perhaps, of a few vague reminiscences the community itself devised a series of incidents which were supposed to manifest the mind of Jesus, and which came to be accepted as historical. This formation of a legend around the figure of Jesus was further assisted by Messianic prophecy. It was assumed that Jesus, as Messiah, had duly fulfilled all that the scriptures had foretold. The predictions were now read as actual history, and were transformed into things that Jesus had done or that had happened to him. What we have in the Gospels is thus nothing but the final precipitation in the form of an historical record of this varied material which had been produced under the later influences.

Now it may be admitted that the record has been affected by the thought and experience of the Christian community. No history has ever been written which did not, in some degree, reflect the interests of the historian's own age. The conflict in ancient Greece or Puritan England reminds him at every point of some contemporary struggle, and unconsciously he puts something of the present into the past. For the early church it was impossible to look back on Jesus with perfect detachment. He was regarded as still living, and sharing in the effort of his people and whatever he had once done merged insensibly in what he was doing now. "To me to live is Christ," says Paul; and he expresses a mood which was familiar to all the early believers. Yet it does not follow that their picture of the historical Jesus was nothing but a shadow, projected from the later conception. Pericles and Cromwell may be presented to us through the atmosphere of our own day, but they were none the less real figures, and what is offered to us as their history is substantially true. In like manner we may accept the record of Jesus. Though it has been modified in the course of transmission it is no less credible than anything else that has come down to us as history. This confidence in the record will only be strengthened when we consider in detail how it seems to have been moulded into its present form.

CHAPTER II

THE HISTORY AND THE MESSAGE

THE Gospels, according to Luke's own description, are the record of "those things which Jesus both did and taught" (Acts 1:1). They have been compared, not inaptly, to the biographies of famous men which were much in vogue in the first century, and of which Plutarch's *Lives* are the classical example. These writings were intended to have at once an historical and an ethical value. The career of the man was clearly outlined, and particular attention was directed to his character. Anecdotes were told of him which were often of little importance in themselves, but which illustrated his disposition and his peculiar virtues. His sayings especially were put on record, as indicating even more plainly than his achievements the manner of man he was. Our Gospels, with their mingling of narrative and anecdote and teaching, are similar to those biographies, and the resemblance may not be wholly accidental; but at the crucial point the comparison breaks down. They are not intended to satisfy curiosity about a remarkable man, nor yet to inculcate virtue by noble example. Their purpose is a religious one. They provide the basis for the Christian message, and their value as history cannot be separated from their religious value.

We have here to reckon with a factor in the Gospels

which might seem fatal, from the start, to their historical character. They are written under the influence of a given belief, and the aim of their writers is to justify that belief. During the generation which followed the death of Jesus he had become the object of Christian faith, and his name was associated with theological and mystical ideas. The record has come to us from that later period when the historical Jesus had been overshadowed by the Christ of faith.[1] Must we not conclude that the facts are so hopelessly confused with the message that they are now lost beyond recovery?

The teaching of Jesus—for this, at least, seems clear from the Gospels—had dealt with the proclamation of the Kingdom of God. The old order was presently to come to an end and give place to a new order, in which the will of God would prevail. Jesus called on men to prepare themselves for this great coming change. He claimed that to him had been granted a unique knowledge of the will of God, which he imparted by deed and saying and parable. Men were to break with their past and follow his new way of life, so that they might be ready for the Kingdom and enter it when it came. Towards the close of his ministry he appears to have declared himself the Messiah, who according to prophecy was to bring in the Kingdom. On the ground of this claim, whether he made it publicly or only within the inner circle of his followers, he was put to death. Henceforward the Messianic aspect of his message became

---

[1]Perhaps the ablest statement of this view is by R. H. Lightfoot, *History and Interpretation in the Gospels.*

central. A community grew up at Jerusalem which accepted his claim, and believed that he would presently return in glory and establish the Kingdom which he had foretold. The thought of the Kingdom was now merged in the Messianic faith. All the thought and activity of the new community were determined by the one belief that the Messiah had now appeared in Jesus of Nazareth, and that he would ensure salvation for his people. This belief was formulated in a definite message which the Christian teachers proclaimed to the world.

The nature of the message can be ascertained with sufficient clearness from a number of passages in the book of Acts and in Paul's Epistles.[2] Jesus had been sent from heaven as the Messiah. He had died to make atonement for sin, and thereby to secure for men that righteousness before God which would enable them to enter his Kingdom. Although he had died he had risen again, and his resurrection had been at once the crowning proof of his Messianic claim and the act whereby he had assumed the full Messianic dignity. He had not only been restored to life but had risen into a new state of being, and from heaven, to which he had now ascended, he would shortly return to judge mankind and to bestow eternal life on those who had put faith in him. On the basis of these convictions a separate group was built up within Judaism. Its members were "the brethren," "the believers," "those who waited for the Lord's

---

[2] C. H. Dodd (*The Apostolic Preaching*) has sought to make out that the primitive beliefs were summarised in a formal statement, resembling a creed, which was employed by all missionaries as the basis of their preaching. The references to the "Kerygma" will hardly admit of this literal interpretation.

coming." They drew into their community not only Palestinian Jews but Jews of foreign origin and finally pure Gentiles; and through the mission of Paul, who was himself a Hellenistic Jew, the new religion became predominantly a Gentile one, and acquired many elements from Pagan worship and philosophy. Of this foreign strain, however, there is little trace in our Gospels. The tradition concerning Jesus appears to have developed, almost wholly, within the Palestinian Church.

It is possible, then, to speak of the Christian message as of something distinct from that of Jesus. His own "gospel" was his announcement of the Kingdom; the church proclaimed that he was himself the Messiah, the Son of God, and this was its "gospel." Paul expressly says that he had determined henceforth not to know Christ after the flesh (II Cor. 5:16). He would concern himself not with Jesus as he had been on earth, but with the exalted Lord through whom we have new life and fellowship with God. In some degree this was also the attitude of those followers of Jesus who, unlike Paul, had personally known him. Their loyalty to him was now inseparable from those beliefs which had grown up since his death, and in this light they now thought of him and worshipped him. According to a view now widely accepted the Gospel tradition arose out of this later estimate of Jesus. He had now ceased to be in any real sense an historical figure. He was invested with all the attributes which prophecy and apocalyptic had bestowed on the Messiah, and his work was interpreted in terms of a theology. What has come to us as his history is nothing but the expression in a concrete form of the speculations of the early church.

Before considering the relation of the Christian message to the history it will be well to clear our minds of a confusion in which a great deal of the recent discussion is involved. It is taken for granted that no history can be true to fact unless it is perfectly objective and impartial. In so far as the historian sets out with preconceived ideas he is deemed incapable of seeing events as they really happened. But if this principle were to be strictly applied, it would go hard with most historians, and especially with those who have always been reckoned the greatest. They invariably approach their subject with some theory of its significance; they seek to present a philosophy as well as a record of fact. This, indeed, is the difference between a mere chronicle and a history. The chronicler has no other aim than to catalogue the events as they occurred—one following another like waves on the beach. History only begins when this work of the annalist is ended. It seeks to discover a cause and a purpose in events that seemed meaningless, and to co-ordinate them by means of some governing idea. By this effort to interpret them the historian does not distort the facts. He rather illuminates them and helps us to see them in their right perspective. This is true of history, and particularly of biography. The writer must know from the outset what his hero was destined to achieve, and consider all that happened to him in relation to that. Things which in themselves were of little consequence may be all-important when they went towards the making of a poet, a discoverer, a liberator. Without this clear conception of the sort of life he is dealing with, a biographer ought never to undertake his task. So it must not be objected to our evangelists that they set out with pre-conceived ideas. Mark declares at the very outset of his Gospel that he thinks of Jesus as the Messiah, the Son of God, and the story that follows has plainly been influenced by that assumption. Must it therefore be set aside as historically worthless? One cannot but wonder sometimes what kind of Gospels some writers are wanting when they reject the present ones as unsatisfactory. Would they have preferred something by a scribe or a Sadducee, who saw nothing in Jesus but a Galilæan carpenter? Would they have wished Mark, when he sat down to write, to divest himself entirely of his Christian ideas and to adopt a purely official attitude, stating the bare facts just as they might have appeared to any casual observer? Such a Gospel would have had a very limited value, even as a record of fact. It might have given more accurate information on some of the external matters in the life of Jesus, but it would have told nothing of the things worth knowing. Books have been written in our own day with the deliberate object of viewing Jesus impartially, and reducing our knowledge of him to the absolute minimum of attested fact. For purely critical purposes these books are useful, but every one feels in reading them that the essential thing has been left out. Jesus, when all is said, has been the most potent force in the world's history; and if this meagre residuum must be taken as everything he remains a pure enigma. Our evangelists may be wrong in thir interpretation, but they have at least faced the problem. They have come to their task with a due sense of the greatness of Jesus, and of the divine power which was somehow working in him. This must not be dismissed as prejudice or illusion. It was the right historical attitude for the understanding of such a life.

The word "theology" ought not, perhaps, to be used at all in connection with our Gospels. Properly speaking the word denotes an effort to explain or justify by reason the truth which is received by faith. In these theological explanations there is always something futile and artificial. As rational beings we are obliged to fall back on them; but our knowledge of God is different in kind from ordinary knowledge, and cannot be grounded in principles derived from it. The evangelists are not theologians. They do not attempt to explain the work of Jesus by any intellectual theory. To be sure they think of him as the Messiah, but this was only the expression of a religious judgment. It meant that he came from God, that in some sense he represented God, that all his words and actions had a divine significance. The Messianic conception was bound up with Jewish apocalyptic and could not be applied to Jesus without, in some measure, changing the character of the historical facts. Yet it was a flexible idea, which had already been construed by Jewish teachers in a great variety of ways.[3] By adopting it the evangelists did not commit them-

[3]Cf. J. Klausner, *Die Messianischen Vorstellungen*; G. F. Moore, *Judaism*, II, 323 ff.

selves to any specific theory of the person of Christ, and its value for them is simply to define the point of view from which they approach the history. They are convinced that Jesus was something more than man, that he not only proclaimed the Kingdom but was essential to its coming, that his life and death were in accordance with a divine plan. This did not involve any theologising of the history. The facts could be recounted as they were, although they were placed in a light which brought out something of their deeper import. In other words, the evangelists had that feeling for Jesus which all reverent souls have had since. They expressed it through the Messianic idea, which was the only one provided for them by the thought of their time. But they were not seeking in this manner to change history into doctrine.

It has been maintained, however, that we must allow for something much more subtle and elaborate in the Messianic teaching of the Gospels. They not only represent Jesus as the Messiah but connect his Messiahship with a theory, to which the facts of the history have been subordinated. What they have given us is not the record but a theological construction of the record. Much has been made in recent years of the idea of the "Messianic secret," which is held to be all-pervasive in the Gospel of Mark.[4] According to this hypothesis Mark thinks of the Messiahship as a mystery, which was concealed in Jesus' life-time, or was only divulged towards the close

[4]The first, and still the most important, statement of the theory is W. Wrede's *Das Messianische Geheimniss* (1901).

to the inner group of disciples. Now and then it was penetrated by the demons, who were beings of a supernatural order; but flesh and blood could not apprehend it, and even the disciples could make little of it until after the Resurrection. In this light we must understand the use, in the later part of Mark's Gospel, of the mysterious title "Son of man." It is meant to indicate that Jesus was the Messiah in no traditional Jewish sense, but by virtue of a hidden divine Sonship. Mark begins with the announcement that this is "the Gospel of Jesus the Messiah, the Son of God," and near the very end he records the centurion's confession, "Truly this was the Son of God." Throughout his work he is the spokesman of some group which held a cryptic doctrine of the Messiahship, and the history is revised in this theological interest. Some elements of fact may be preserved, but they are treated merely as the adumbration of a hidden truth in which the Christian message essentially consists.[5]

Now it is difficult to credit Mark with this abstruse doctrinal purpose, which would certainly be missed by his early readers, as by every one since, except some ingenious critics in the twentieth century. If he had wished to promulgate a new theory he would have done so more explicitly; and it is more natural to suppose that he works with the Messianic idea as it was commonly understood in the church of his day. If he sought to introduce a new and more profound Christology his intention was not perceived by the other two evangelists,

[5] R. H. Lighfoot, *History and Interpretation*, Ch. III.

who apparently thought him defective at this very point. Again and again they find it necessary to correct his language, as wanting in due reverence for Jesus. Writing as they do in the next generation they are aware that Mark reflects the attitude of a time when the tradition had not been fully correlated with the message. There is, indeed, no reason why that secrecy on which Mark insists should not correspond with an historical fact. Jesus had arrived at the conviction that he was Messiah with many misgivings—conscious, it may be, that his calling was not wholly in keeping with the prophetic hope. Nearly to the end he was seeking for more certainty, and was unwilling to commit himself by a public proclamation. He knew, moreover, that as soon as his claim was disclosed he would cease to be master of his own actions, and might be hurried into imprudent courses. No theology is needed to explain an aspect of the history which in itself is perfectly intelligible. Jesus withheld his secret because he wished as long as possible to keep himself free, and to make his declaration at his own time and in his own way.

What Mark affirms, from the beginning to the end of his Gospel, is simply the fact that Jesus was the Messiah. This was the cardinal Christian belief, and in proof of it the evangelist tells of the miracles, the testimony offered by angels and demons, the convincing power of the teaching, the faith awakened in the disciples, the manner of the death and resurrection. There is probably no passage in Mark's Gospel which has not some bearing on the Messianic belief, and to this extent it may be said that the writer is concerned not only with facts but with their import. He lies open to the suspicion which attaches to all historians who have written with a purpose—Thucydides, Tacitus, Macaulay, Carlyle and countless others. In their version of events we have constantly to allow for a motive, but this does not mean that the events themselves are doubtful. If the writer were merely inventing, or repeating vague hearsay, he would defeat his own intention, which is to support the view he holds by admitted facts. At most we can only object to Mark that he has selected his facts and put his own construction on them; and the same is true of the other evangelists. Their procedure is much the same as that which Luke has followed in his supplementary work, the book of Acts. His view of the task and character of the early church is different from that which we might gather from Paul's Epistles; but it is obtained by careful selection and skilful changes of emphasis. The facts themselves are substantially the same in Luke's account and in Paul's.

It is a fundamental principle in all enquiry that fact and interpretation ought not to be confused with each other. A theory may be totally wrong, and yet may be based on observations which cannot be disputed. We reject the Ptolemaic astronomy, but the phenomena which it seeks to explain are none the less real. We may question the opinions of Thucydides on Athenian policy, but the conduct of Athens during the war was no doubt as he describes it. This distinction must never be forgotten in our criticism of the Gospels. It may be that mistaken meanings have been read by the evangelists into their account of Jesus, but this must not affect our judgment of the history. There is no reason to question that the things recorded are authentic, although at some points we can trace the ideas of a later time. The evangelists are interpreters as well as historians, and it need not be assumed that the interpretation has produced, or even seriously modified, the facts.

It is necessary, however, to enquire more closely into the relation of the Gospel history to the message which it is intended to support. We know that in the age following the death of Jesus there grew up certain beliefs concerning him which apparently had little connection with anything he had actually done. The Apostles' Creed, in which these beliefs were firmly summarised, passes at once from the birth of Jesus to his death. No mention is made of the events between, for it was felt that Christianity essentially consisted in the acceptance of that salvation which had come through Jesus. To believe in him it was no more necessary to know his history than to study the career of Euclid before you can trust his conclusions. Paul himself refuses to know Christ after the flesh. It was enough to be assured that Christ was now Lord, and had won redemption for his people.

A message was thus proclaimed by the church, which might seem to stand by itself, with little connection except in name with the historical figure of Jesus. Many theories have been put forward as to how this message had come into being. According to one view it had sprung out of Jewish apocalyptic. The Christ whom the church believed in was the Messiah of the apocalyptic hope, who had now come to be vaguely identified with the prophet of Nazareth. Others would find the true origins of Christianity in some esoteric school of Jewish thought, either in Palestine itself or in the more speculative Judaism of the Dispersion. Or they would trace it directly to Hellenistic influences which may have acted, almost from the beginning, on the community which formed itself at Jerusalem. It is indeed more than probable that a number of forces co-operated in the making of early Christianity. Correspondences may be found in the New Testament to almost all the religious conceptions which were current in the first century, and in many cases this can hardly have been fortuitous. But these extraneous influences came into effect only in the formulation of the message. They do not account for its substance, and much less do they explain how it came to be associated with Jesus. This, when all is said, is the real problem.

It is not enough to say that by the confluence of many streams of thought a new religion evolved itself, and somehow found its missionaries in the obscure Christian sect. Why did it do so? This cannot be accounted for by any theory of happy coincidence. There must have been something in the Christian tradition itself which enabled it to press into its service all that could be contributed by the miscellaneous thinking of the time. It has been argued that Paul takes his real departure from the Jewish apocalyptic idea of the Messiah. He connects it with the Christian faith in Jesus, but all the time it is the Messiah of Jewish speculation in whom Paul's thought is centred, and around whom he weaves his whole message of salvation. But his procedure, when we examine it, is just the opposite. He starts always from certain facts, received, as he tells us, from the church before him. Christ had appeared and had died for men and through him God had revealed himself and had done for us what we could not do ourselves. Everything in Paul that is speculative and theological, everything that is brought in from apocalyptic and Hellenistic thought, is used only to explain those facts which were given in the Christian tradition. Nothing could be further from the truth than to ground the message of Paul in ideas which serve only for its doctrinal expression.

What is demonstrably true of Paul is no less true of the Christian teaching generally. It cannot be maintained that the message came first, and then produced a history which aimed at justifying it. This, on the face of it, is incredible, and is contrary to all the evidence. It was the history which created the message, although it may be that when the message, under various influences, had assumed a doctrinal form, it re-acted on the history out of which it had grown. Facts were now conceived, not entirely as they had been, but in the light of doctrines which they had suggested. The Ptolemaic astronomy, to take our previous instance, was founded on the observed motions of the stars; but when once the theory had been accepted no one could regard those motions except in the light of it. So in history there is always a tendency to credit a great man with the conscious pursuance of aims which were only implicit in his work. The wars of Cæsar are explained as waged deliberately for the creation of the later empire; the thought of Socrates as inspired by those conceptions to which it eventually gave rise. This has doubtless happened, to some extent, in the record of the life of Jesus. When our Gospels were written the church had reflected on its message, and had learned to express it in terms which might have appeared strange to Jesus himself. The later conceptions could not but affect the minds of the evangelists as they dealt with the records. They believed in the message as now proclaimed by the church, and tried to find confirmation of it in the history. But from this it does not follow that the history was dependent on the message.

Much of the modern criticism of the Gospels would seem, indeed, to be based on a misconception. It is assumed that the message and the record were, from the outset, quite different things, and that the record owed its existence to a kind of afterthought.[6] For a generation or more the message had been proclaimed as something by itself—that Jesus was the Messiah sent from God, and that by faith in him men might enter into fellowship with God and obtain his salvation. Then a time came when Christians began to ask themselves, "Who was this Jesus who wrought such great things for mankind?" In answer to this demand for more definite

[6]This position is tacitly adopted by most of the exponents of *Formgeschichte*.

knowledge of him our Gospels appeared. The memory of Jesus had now grown dim. Those who knew him personally had passed away, and the church, pre-occupied with its message, had taken no care to enquire into his history. But the practice now began of collecting the stray reminiscences which still happened to survive. They had grown faded, and were mingled with doubtful legend, but such as they were they were put into writing and finally gathered into our Gospels. What purported to be a history was thus added as a pendant to the message.

There are two great weaknesses in this theory. On the one hand it rests on the assumption that the making of a record was a late development, never even contemplated until the beliefs of the church had been fully defined. If this were so, it would indeed follow that the Gospels can have only a secondary value. There would always be a suspicion that they merely reflected the later teaching, and even if it could be shown that they contained elements of good tradition, this would have to be regarded as irrelevant. The substance of Christian belief would be the message itself. These reminiscences of Jesus would at best be a mere appendix, intended to satisfy a reasonable curiosity as to the earthly life of this divine Person, who was the object of faith. It can be proved, however, that the record was not a late development. Our Gospels may have been written in the second or third generation after Christ; the earliest of them certainly dates from a time subsequent to the theology of Paul. But they are made from material which existed, even in a written form, in a much earlier time. They can be traced back to a tradition which must have been current in the church in Palestine almost from the beginning. Whatever its origin, therefore, the record was not due to the research of later teachers, who felt the need of supplementing in this manner the beliefs of the church. Nor was it something extraneous, grafted on to a message which had grown up apart from it and had taken definite shape before it was added. Both the record and the message went back to primitive days. If they were different they had always been inseparable. There was never a time when the church was neglectful of the life of Jesus and thought only of the message.

On the other hand, this theory leaves out of account what was always the distinctive thing about Christianity. In other religions the personality of the founder is non-essential. Very little is known of Moses, Buddha, Zoroaster, and even if it were proved that they had never lived at all, the religions which accept them as prophets would remain the same. All that matters is the teaching attributed to those great names, and it would be just as valid if it were connected with others. Jesus, however, is central to his religion, which would at once lose all its meaning if he were withdrawn. When Paul was asked in a moment of crisis to sum up in one word the way of salvation, he could only answer "Believe in the Lord Jesus Christ." This faith in Christ is the vital thing in Christianity, and it cannot be resolved into faith in a principle, or a symbol, or an imaginary being. It means, in the last resort, that the power of God was manifested in very deed through a human life. Jesus, for the Christian, is the unassailable fact on which his faith is based, and which gives it certainty. This demand for faith in Christ was not a later element in Christianity, introduced by Paul or some other innovator. It was the substance of the religion from the first. The very mark of a Christian was baptism in the name of Christ, —that is, a personal surrender whereby you became a servant of Christ. This loyalty to him was the one thing that mattered in the Christian life, and expressed itself in the confession "Jesus is Lord," which for a long time was the only creed of the church.

So by its nature Christianity involved a knowledge of Jesus. Faith in him was impossible without some clear conception of what he was. It was not enough to say "Believe in Jesus, who appeared on earth as Messiah and has now ascended to heaven." The question would at once be raised, "Where and when did he appear? How did he show himself to be Messiah?" A missionary at the present day needs always to lead up to his message by some account of the Gospel history. Much of his teaching consists in nothing else than in repeating the simple facts, and making them vivid and concrete. The call to believe in Jesus has no meaning whatever until Jesus is thus presented as a living personality. It is not conceivable that the primitive missionary can have followed any different method. Since his aim was to awaken faith in Jesus he must have told what he knew of Jesus; he must have been far more explicit than the modern missionary, speaking as he did to Jews and

Pagans who were often misinformed on the facts. Much has been made of Paul's refusal to know Christ after the flesh, and of his comparative silence, throughout the Epistles, on the story of the earthly life. Do we not here have evidence that Paul, at any rate, made little of the historical life and threw the whole emphasis on the message? But Paul implies in this very passage (II Cor. 5:16) that too much attention was commonly given to the life. The ordinary Christian was content to remember what Jesus had once been, and had no desire to press forward and know him as still living. Paul confesses that he himself, before he had learned the full scope of the revelation, had been satisfied with the historical knowledge. His endeavour now is to build on that foundation and attain to the larger conception of Christ.

Here, then, we are to seek the true relation of the Gospel history to the Gospel message. The whole enquiry has been vitiated by the idea that the two things must be kept separate. It is assumed that on the one hand there were certain beliefs held by Jesus' followers, and on the other hand a tradition about Jesus himself. The historical content of the Gospels is thus arrived at by a method of subtraction. All the theological elements have to be squeezed out of the narrative, and we are then left with a residuum, which may possibly consist of historical fact. At every point the two interests must be carefully distinguished—Jesus as an actual Person and Jesus as the object of faith. Only when this is done can we hope to get behind the Gospels to the history.

It is along this line of reasoning that the narrative is set aside, as merely an outgrowth of the later message or an appendix which came in the course of time to be attached to it; but surely another view is possible. The record was not something added to the message, but was itself the message in its original form. At a later day the church expressed its beliefs in theological language, and these abstract statements were accepted, as containing the substance of Christian faith. In the earlier time the account of what Jesus had said and done took the place of formal doctrine. Here were the facts which represented the new message, and the hearer might make of them what he would. He was not asked to assent to any creed, but merely to believe, on the word of those who had witnessed it, that the life of Jesus had been lived in this manner. The record itself was held to be sufficient. Those who laid it to heart would perceive that Jesus was indeed the Messiah, and that salvation must be by faith in him. The teacher would certainly do his best to make that conclusion evident, but his chief business was to impress on his hearers the Christian facts.

When it is thus considered the record is no mere supplement to the message, but the message itself in its earlier form. Our evangelists belonged to the generation after Paul, and perhaps availed themselves of ideas which had come in through Paul and other thinkers; but their aim has been to gather up and to present in orderly fashion the primitive traditions. They preserve to us what was taught in the church at the time when it had no other teaching. Their record, so far from growing out of the later message, was the material out of which the message was formed. It gives us the things known about Jesus, and from these the church proceeded to construct its doctrine of his Person and work. An illustration may be taken from the Lord's Supper, the observance of which, according to Paul's testimony, had always been modelled on the original rite. In this instance an act of Jesus was not merely recounted but re-enacted. It stood for the solemn pledge which Jesus had made to his people, and was therefore repeated, in a visible, impressive form, at every church meeting. Already in the time of Paul the observance was interpreted doctrinally, and it gradually became the centre of a whole mystical theology. But in the primitive days the church was satisfied with the repetition of the rite itself. The message intended by it was conveyed by the presentation to mind and senses of what Jesus himself had done, while he was still with men. This one act of Jesus was dramatised; others were only recounted. But the narrative had a religious value, similar to that of the re-enactment of the Supper. By receiving the tradition of Jesus his followers received his message, which was inseparable, in the last resort, from the facts of his life.

One thing, indeed, has always to be borne in mind—that the closing events of the life over-shadowed everything that had gone before. In our present Gospels practically nothing is told us of the years preceding the Baptism, with which the Messianic career of Jesus had begun; and in a similar manner the ministry itself is eclipsed by the great events which crowned the Messianic work. Nearly half the space in each of our Gospels is occupied with the closing week of Jesus' life. All the rest is treated as a preparation for the fulfilment, which is kept steadily in view from the beginning. From this it is sometimes argued that the whole narrative which leads up to the Passion lies open to suspicion. We know that in Paul's teaching the death of Jesus is everything. He tells us himself that he preached Christ crucified—that he held up before his hearers, as in a vivid picture, the scene of Christ dying for man's salvation (Gal. 3:1). Paul, it must never be forgotten, was only one of the early teachers, and there is no ground for supposing that in his general method he differed from the others. They also would throw the emphasis on the death and the incidents related to it; and this presumption is borne out by the place given in the Gospels to the Passion story. Must we not conclude that originally it stood by itself—the one part of the narrative which had come down from the primitive time, and that all the rest was added later, from vague reminiscence or pure fancy, to give a semblance of completeness to what would otherwise have been a fragment?

Such a theory is at first sight plausible. Since the Christian message was concerned supremely with the death of Christ, this was the one part of the historical record which needed to be constantly repeated, and the church would grow careless of everything else in the story so long as this one essential element was preserved. To this it may be answered that at the time when our Gospels were written an account of the ministry was already an integral part of the tradition. The motive which weighed with the evangelists had also affected the authors of their documents, and must have been operative from the first. It had always been felt that the later part of the history could not be understood without the earlier. The record of the death contained the essential message, but it could not stand alone. Those who listened to it would inevitably ask many questions. What had Jesus done before that last week in Jerusalem? How had he drawn on himself the hostility of priests and scribes? What evidence had he given before his Messianic death that he was in truth the Messiah? We perceive, as we read the Gospels now, that the life and the death are all of one piece, and that otherwise the death itself would lose its significance. This would be no less apparent to those who first listened to the Christian teachers. There must always have been some introduction to the Passion story, explaining who Jesus was and illustrating his aims and character by things he had done. The more men heard of his death the more they would desire to learn how he had lived, and the two parts of the record would merge together. This was the history of Jesus, and at the same time the proclamation which the church offered to the world.

It is thus by no accident that the writings which give us the narrative of Jesus' life are now known as the "Gospels."[7] This name, one might think, would apply

---

[7] As first used by Ignatius (letters to Philadelphia and Smyrna) the term "Gospel" seems to denote the account of Jesus—not some particular writing in which it is contained.

more properly to the later New Testament books, in which we have no mere chronicle but the message itself, the clear exposition of God's purpose, as manifested in Christ. Yet men have always turned from the exposition to the record, and have felt that here they discover the true "gospel." This was already realised by the primitive church. Its message did not consist in some doctrine about Jesus but in the plain account of how he had lived and died. Through these facts he had made his revelation.

In this connection it will be well to consider the place of the Fourth Gospel in the development of the tradition. The modern discussion has based itself, in large measure, on the character of this Gospel, in which the facts are interpreted by certain doctrinal ideas which tend, at every turn, to modify or displace them. History and theology are fused together. For this reason it was generally admitted, twenty or thirty years ago, that the Fourth Gospel was on a different footing from the other three; but this is now denied by many scholars. They hold that John is in direct succession to Mark, Matthew and Luke, and exhibits in a more advanced and explicit form that work on the tradition which had been continually going on.[8] In him we see the process of Gospel-making in its final outcome, so that he provides us with the clue to the Synoptic Gospels and the documents behind them. The aims and methods which had hither-

---

[8]This is the underlying thesis of R. H. Lightfoot's *History and Interpretation in the Gospels*. M. Goguel (*Vie de Jésus*) regards the Fourth Gospel as mainly theological, but holds that it is based, like the Synoptics, on genuine historical documents.

to been partially concealed are now disclosed in a manner that cannot be mistaken. Following this clue we can perceive that Mark, which at first sight appears to be a purely historical record, was written in a theological interest. It mingles interpretation with fact; it freely adapts the history to the existing needs and problems of the church. Everything that can be predicated of John's Gospel must hold equally true of the others, which were tending in the same direction.

Now it cannot be denied that in this view there is a measure of truth which needs to be recognised. The author of the Fourth Gospel took up the work of his predecessors. He seeks like them to record the life of Jesus, and probably made use, not only of the Synoptic narratives, but of other historical material of undoubted value. He is conscious, like the other evangelists, that the Christian message cannot stand alone but must be linked with the things that actually happened.[9]

At the same time it remains true, as even the casual reader has always been aware, that the Fourth Gospel is different from the others. While it is of the same family it marks a new departure, and any attempt to explain the Synoptists from John can only lead to confusion. This becomes apparent when we consider some of the distinctive features of this Gospel.

(1) It is not a compilation of earlier documents but a new and independent work. We feel that the author

---

[9] M. Goguel, in his recent *Vie de Jésus* (translation, *Life of Jesus*), discovers behind the Fourth Gospel a document of primary historical value. This idea is pressed too far, but some recognition of the authentic character of certain parts of the Johannine record was more than due.

has read and assimilated a number of previous writings, and has then laid them aside. His object is not merely to hand down the tradition but to pour it into a new mould and re-fashion it.

(2) Though almost certainly a Jew, he is a Hellenist, and works with the Alexandrian method. It was the aim of the Rabbis to keep faithful to tradition, preserving the data of their predecessors with the necessary comments and elucidations. Alexandrian teachers went back to the original scripture and sought with the help of allegory to fill it with new meaning. The church in Palestine had followed the example of the Rabbinical schools, maintaining as far as possible the tradition of what Jesus had said and done. John seeks, like the Alexandrians, to penetrate the hidden import of the historical facts. Between him and the Synoptists there is the same kind of difference as between Philo and the Rabbis.

(3) The Fourth Gospel is controversial. It deals with the Christian teaching not only in its intrinsic character but in its contrast with Judaism and Gnosticism. There may be controversial motives in the Synoptic Gospels, but they arise for the most part from differences of opinion within the community itself, and do not affect the central principles of Christian faith. The Synoptic writers, moreover, are content to indicate their own views by means of selection and emphasis, and hold carefully to the facts as recorded in their sources. With John the controversial motive is of primary importance. In order to bring out more clearly the Christian

answer to what he conceives to be error, he does not hesitate to take liberties with the facts.

(4) The historical life is subordinated in the Fourth Gospel to the Logos doctrine, and this involves a theological treatment far more drastic than in the other Gospels. The conception of Messiahship was not, in the proper sense, a doctrinal one. It was historical in its origin and lent itself, without undue strain, to the interpretation of a history. Little was required to prove that Jesus was the Messiah except to show that at one point and another he gave fulfilment to Old Testament prediction; and this could be done without any serious departure from the known circumstances of his life. Not only so, but the Synoptic writers work on the assumption that in his lifetime the Messiahship of Jesus was latent, and was not fully disclosed until after the Resurrection. This idea, as we have seen, has in recent times been construed as a subtle theological one, elaborated by Mark under the guise of history. But it may more reasonably be explained as Mark's device for affirming the Messianic belief and yet presenting the life historically. Jesus was the Messiah, but this truth, in its higher significance, was only perceived afterwards. The events of the life could be viewed apart from it, as they appeared at the time to the imperfect vision of men. For the Fourth evangelist Jesus was the Logos, and in all his action he made this Logos nature apparent. "He manifested forth his glory." His teaching all centred on the oracular "I am," with which he asserts his prerogative as Son of God. This conception of Jesus in-

volves the re-writing of the history. It is no longer sufficient to record the traditions; they have to be revised and transformed, in the light of Logos theory.

(5) The Fourth Gospel is consciously the transcript of a mystical experience, as well as of a history. Two conceptions are always present to the writer's mind—that of Jesus as he lived on earth, and that of Jesus as he now dwells invisibly in the hearts of believers. By his death he was set free from the limitations of space and time, and so returned to abide with his people forever. His earthly life had been only the foreshadowing and the guarantee of this other and deeper fellowship with him which would ensue. It is not too much to say that the real interest of John is in this inward manifestation of Christ. He keeps it in his mind and is trying to describe it all the time that he traces out the earthly history.

The Synoptists, it may be answered, are also conscious of a permanent value in the life, and for this reason preserve incidents which may seem, at times, to have little import in themselves. But the value which they attribute to the life is of a different kind. They think of Jesus as setting the great example, as teaching the fixed principles of Christian action, as bringing the revelation of God's will, as accomplishing by his death the Messianic redemption. His work for men had a permanent value because it was achieved once for all, and thus gave the Christian religion its permanent basis. For John the work had a meaning for all times because it would repeat itself endlessly in the experience of faith. As Jesus had lived with his first disciples he would continue to live, making the same revelation and doing the same deeds under ever-changing forms. It is evident that a history so conceived is of a different order from that in the Synoptic Gospels. Its object is not the preserving of a tradition but the merging of this tradition in a mystical experience.

Thus it is misleading to speak of all the Gospels as linked together in the same succession, and to assume that in Mark we must look for all the characteristics which we find in John. By an assumption of this kind we miss the true significance alike of the Synoptic Gospels and of the Fourth. We construe in a purely external sense those great utterances of the Fourth Gospel which tell of the living Christ, who comes back as an inward presence to those who love him. We read theology into those Synoptic narratives which are of infinite value because they are history. They do not set before us some fancied interpretation of the Christian message but the message itself, as it was given through the actual life of Jesus Christ on earth.

CHAPTER III

THE TRADITION IN CHURCH WORSHIP

I⊤ is almost an axiom with many modern scholars
that the Gospels arose, almost of their own accord, out
of the life of the Christian community.[1] During the
whole of that dark period before anything was written,
reminiscences of Jesus had been current among the various groups of believers in Palestine, and had been used
in the common worship and in the ordering of the common activities. By this constant employment they had
acquired new forms and meanings. They had been
adapted and readapted to changing circumstances, until
they lost their original shape, like pebbles which are
finally worn smooth by the action of the tides. Many
critics would go a step farther. They would hold that the
tradition was not only modified by its use in the community, but was in some measure created. When examined
in detail it is found to reflect conditions which were not
those of Jesus' lifetime, but which answer to those
which existed, or may have existed, in the early church.[2]
Must we not infer that the Christian society, in the effort to maintain itself, evolved principles and ideas

[1]The position is well stated by Kundsin: "It has become increasingly clear
that the Gospels and their sources are primarily the expression and reflection
of the faith and life of the early Christian churches which produced them."
(*Form Criticism*, edited by F. C. Grant, p. 81.)
[2]*Cf.* S. J. Case, *Social Origins of Christianity*.

which it made authoritative by ascribing them to its
Founder? At the most it can have derived from him
only the bare suggestion of much that it put forward as
his word or example. The tradition as it finally emerged
from that period of silent growth in the community was
mainly the product of the community itself.

This theory undoubtedly contains some elements of
truth. Our Gospels go back to records which were preserved in the church, and the church preserved them
for a practical purpose. It had accepted Jesus as its
Master, and looked to him for guidance in the urgent
difficulties which it encountered as it felt its way along
untried paths. The memories of Jesus which survived
in the church would, for the most part, be those which
appeared most relevant to its own problems, and to
this extent the church was an all-important factor in the
making of the tradition. If it did not create those records of Jesus, at least it was the sieve through which
they had to pass, and which selected some things in
preference to others. More than this may be granted.
In the endeavour to make a word or action of Jesus
fully applicable to a new situation, some turn would
occasionally be given to it which altered its character.
There is a passage in First Corinthians in which this
modification takes place, as it were, before our very
eyes. Paul has occasion to quote Jesus' teaching on divorce: "To the married I command, yet not I but the
Lord; Let not the wife depart from her husband (but
if she depart let her remain unmarried or be reconciled
to her husband) and let not the husband put away his

wife (I Cor. 7:10, 11). The parenthesis is Paul's own addition, but he combines it with the saying quoted, in such a way that Jesus becomes responsible for the rule which must henceforth be observed. A still more striking example is to be found in the passage on the erring brother, as reported by Luke and by Matthew. Luke gives the saying in what is doubtless its original form. "If thy brother sin rebuke him, and if he repent forgive him (Lk. 17:3). In Matthew this is transformed into a rule of ecclesiastical order: "If thy brother sin, rebuke him between thyself and him alone; but if he does not listen, take with thyself one man or two; and if he will not hear them tell it to the church, and if he will not hear the church, let him be to thee as the heathen or the publican" (Mt. 18:15–17). Here we can see the community (still on Palestinian ground, as is evident from the concluding words) doubtful as to how it should deal with a recalcitrant member. It takes a saying of Jesus which is too general to meet the special case, and expands it into a definite rule of church discipline. Something of this kind has no doubt happened repeatedly in the Gospels. There is hardly a paragraph in which we may not suspect a later adaptation. Sometimes it is so considerable that the underlying words of Jesus can only be conjectured. Sometimes it is nothing but a blur, like that of finger-marks on an object that has been handled. The critical reader soon learns to make a constant allowance for these changes to which the record has been subject.

It cannot be admitted, however, that the Gospels are

mainly the work of the Christian community. This theory, which has won a great vogue in recent years, may be set down partly to mere looseness of thinking. Since the Gospels came into existence, and we cannot find out exactly how, we are content to say that they grew up in some way out of the common mind of the church. The theory is the more acceptable as it answers to our modern faith in the mysterious virtue of a crowd. We trace everything back to mass movement. We regard it almost as a law of nature that if plenty of people can be got together they will be sure to incubate something great. Jesus himself cannot have originated his religion; neither can it be credited to any individual teachers. But when we assume a community, made up of very ordinary people but a great number of them, putting their minds together, everything seems to become possible. Now the truth is that a community, as such, never produces anything. For whatever it decides or does some one man is ultimately responsible, although the consent of the many gives the necessary weight to his action. A group is never creative. Left to itself it only stands still; and in all ages this has been the fatal drawback to any type of society that is strictly communal. Least of all in matters of the spirit is anything produced by the group. We speak of an ancient song or ballad as made by the people; but this is only our way of saying that we cannot name the author. There was not a village crowd which broke out into the song spontaneously: some one made it, just as surely as Milton made *Paradise Lost*. In the same manner every religion, even the crudest, has come, in the last resort, out of the soul of some one man. We may call it tribal or primitive, and so contrast it with the religions that had definite founders. But the distinction is unreal, and serves no other purpose than to mask our ignorance. Behind every religion there lies some revelation, made not to the tribe but to some nameless prophet. It is necessary to insist on these obvious facts, because in our time the notion of communal activity is so often employed, even by serious thinkers, to do duty for real investigation into the sources of ideas and movements. Anything that cannot be explained is now attributed to the communal mind, much as all strange phenomena are put down among primitive peoples to some hidden agency into which it is impious to enquire. This mode of thought has found its way into the study of Christian origins, and is posing, for the moment, as the only one that is truly scientific. Everything was the work of the community. All that was new in Christian teaching and institutions sprang somehow out of the general mind, and in this way also the Gospel tradition must be explained. So much has been made of this strange theory that it is necessary to consider in some detail what was the real function of the church in the making of the Gospels.

There can be little doubt that the community in question was that which grew up in Palestine, and was comparatively untouched by Gentile influences. The Gospels, probably all of them, were written on Gentile soil and were based on Greek sources, drawn up in churches which had Greek for their language. But in the Greek it is not difficult to trace forms of expression which betray an Aramaic original, and the whole colouring both of style and contents is Palestinian. This is true also of the general background of the records. If they had originated in any foreign land it would have been impossible to reproduce with such fidelity the Palestinian setting of custom, scenery, religious practice, social and political conditions.

It has been suggested that at least some part of the record may have been formed at Antioch, where an important church was founded within a very few years of Jesus' death.[3] This is conceivable, but there is nothing in the Gospels themselves which lends support to the theory. If the accounts of Jesus' teaching had taken shape in a church planted in a great Gentile city, we should have expected some reference to the special problems which beset Christianity in such an environment. When Paul writes his first Epistle to the Corinthians he is conscious in almost every verse of the heathen surroundings in which the Christian message has now to work, and presents it in its bearing on these changed conditions. Nothing of the kind is indicated in the sayings of Jesus preserved in our Gospels. The people addressed are those to whom the Law is the norm of righteousness; the sins condemned are not the gross heathen vices but pride, hypocrisy, self-seeking, reli-

[3]B. H. Streeter (*The Four Gospels*, 400 ff.) adduces strong reasons for regarding Antioch as the birthplace of the Gospel of Matthew. This does not mean, however, that the tradition embodied in Matthew was formed at Antioch.

gious parade—sins which were only too familiar in
Judaism but for which the Gentiles had hardly a name.
In like manner there is no hint of the controversies
which agitated the Gentile churches, or of the criticisms against which they had to defend their faith. All
the horizons are those of a community confined to Palestine. This is the more remarkable as the Gospels in
their present form were undoubtedly composed in the
Greek language for the Gentile church. It may be inferred that the records from which they are made were
not only of Palestinian origin, but had been so long
and intimately connected with Palestine that their
character could not be altered.

The community, then, to which we owe the Gospels
was that which existed in Palestine in the generation
which followed the death of Jesus. This community
is only known to us from the scanty notices in the book
of Acts and a few incidental references in Paul's Epistles. Our information would be more extensive if we
could take into account those passages in the Gospels
themselves which seem to bear on the later church; but
their evidence must be disregarded since our very object is to discover whether it is really present. Gospel
criticism has too often reached its conclusions by a
method which is found, on examination, to be nothing
else than reasoning in a circle. The circumstances of
the church are deduced from the Gospel narrative, and
then it is shown, without much difficulty, that the narrative conforms to those circumstances. It will be well
to confine ourselves, at least in the first instance, to the

positive knowledge, however meagre, which may be gathered from independent testimony.

We know, then, that a community of Jesus' followers was formed, after his death, at Jerusalem, and gradually threw out offshoots into the surrounding country. We hear most of Christian activity in the larger towns, particularly to the west of Jerusalem and along the seaboard. Strangely enough Galilee falls out of the picture, and it may be inferred that for some reason the mission had failed to prosper in the region of its origin.[4] Our record of the Galilæan ministry might have been fuller if the church had established itself more firmly in that part of the country where Jesus had chiefly laboured. It is doubtful, however, whether any of the outlying communities contributed much to the record. Unlike the Pauline churches, each of which had a standing and character of its own, those in Palestine were dominated by Jerusalem. The country was a small one, and the mission as it spread could easily be controlled from the centre. Jerusalem, moreover, had a unique prestige as the holy city and the home of the leading Apostles. All evangelising seems to have been carried out under their direction, and by personal visits from time to time they maintained their hold on the daughter churches. When Paul contrasts his fatherly attitude with the authority claimed as their due by

[4]An interesting theory has lately been advanced by E. Lohmeyer (*Galiläa und Jerusalem*) that a Christian community, disregarded in our New Testament, grew up in Galilee, under the supervision of the Lord's own family. The theory is highly conjectural; and against it there is the indubitable fact that James, the Lord's brother, was head of the church at Jerusalem.

other Apostles, we may catch a side-light on the conditions which were accepted as normal in the Palestinian mission. Jerusalem was everything, and the other communities were made to feel that they had no initiative, and no valid existence apart from the ruling church. The Jewish emissaries, when they sought to win over Paul's Gentile converts, relied on this primacy of Jerusalem. They took for granted that everywhere, as in Palestine itself, the word of the mother church was final. All this must be borne in mind when we consider the formation of the Gospel record. It is often assumed that each of the little communities in Palestine had its own particular tradition, and that our Gospels resulted from a blending of these diverse accounts. Such a view can hardly be reconciled with the given situation. All the local churches on Jewish territory were connected in the closest manner with each other, and had been instructed by the same body of teachers. We have to do, not with a number of traditions gathered from different quarters, but with the one tradition which had developed within the circle of Jerusalem.

It is therefore in this mother church that we must seek the influences which went towards the moulding of the record; and our data for the most part are of a purely external nature. We hear of conflicts with the Jewish authorities, of increases in numbers, of continued poverty, of changes in leadership. It is only incidentally that any light is thrown on the activities of the church and the character of its piety and beliefs. We can gather, however, that it was made up of very

diverse elements. Within a year or two of its foundation the native and foreign-born members were sharply
divided, and at a later time Paul encountered much
difference of opinion when he sought a decision on the
validity of his teaching. Under the leadership of James
the mother church appears to have steadily grown more
Jewish in its outlook, and finally to have parted company with Gentile Christianity. We can gather, too,
that it continued to hold firmly to apocalyptic beliefs,
and perhaps the poverty under which it always suffered
was due, in some measure, to the stubborn expectation
that the end was immediately at hand. It is sometimes
assumed that with its bias towards the Law and the Jewish apocalyptic hopes, the church in Palestine was nationalistic, and regarded Jesus as in some literal sense
the Messiah who would deliver Israel. Some passages
in the Gospels might seem to point to this attitude to
the Messiahship, and they have been singled out as
typical of the prevailing mood. It would indeed be natural that many of the Palestinian Christians would
cling to literal Messianic ideas long after the Gentile
church had discarded them; but the general sentiment
cannot have been a narrowly nationalistic one. We know
that the Christians in Jerusalem refused to participate in
the great revolt, and withdrew in a body to the region
beyond Jordan on the outbreak of the war. This action,
we may be sure, was consistent with the position they
had always taken. If they stood for a Christianity which
did not relinquish its hold on Judaism they still recognised that Jesus had taught no mere political religion.

Their hope was for a Kingdom of God such as Jesus himself had proclaimed.

Occasional glimpses of this community are not wanting in aspects of its life which had little to do with external or dogmatic interests. Meetings for prayer were held in private houses, the sick and poor were diligently cared for, the brethren associated daily at common meals, they shared their possessions, they rejoiced to suffer for Christ's cause. Luke, in the early chapters of Acts, may have idealised the primitive conditions, but he cannot have done so unless he had facts to build on. It was remembered in the later age, when most other things had been forgotten, that the early church had been animated by a fervid spirit of devotion and brotherly love. Men and women, in their little house-gatherings, had waited from day to day for the Lord's coming, and the Kingdom, which he was presently to bring in, was more real to them than the actual world. This side of the church's activity must never be forgotten when we try to realise the conditions under which the Gospel record was preserved and transmitted.

One fact can hardly be emphasised too much—that their association in the church covered the whole life of those early believers. This is apparent from the letters of Paul, who takes for granted that all the interests of his readers are controlled by their fellowship together as Christians. On stated occasions they meet in small groups or as a whole community for purposes of worship, but at all times they feel themselves united in Christian living. Although they must needs have intercourse with the outer world they constitute, as far as possible, a self-contained society, watching over each other's needs, settling all differences among themselves, marrying within their own circle, making "brotherly love" their chief moral aim. The common worship was only the religious expression of that unity in thought and action which embraced the whole of their life.

This effort to include all interests in the Christian society must have been even more pronounced in Palestine than among the Gentiles. For the Jews, to an extent unknown in other nations, religion meant everything; and no distinction was made between religious and secular activities. Not only so, but in that first generation, when they were looking hourly for the return of Christ, the believers had a single purpose in their lives. Prayer and action and social duty were all fused together. It is the weakness of much recent enquiry that everything is considered from the side of worship in its purely ceremonial sense.[5] Because the Gospels are religious books it is assumed that they grew out of religious practice and must be related in every detail to the cult and doctrine of the church. But it must be remembered that religion for the primitive Christians was life in its whole extent. Just as the law of Moses was concerned not only with sacrifice and the Sabbath but with marriage and property and agriculture and all the business of living, so the Christian demand in-

---

[5] M. Dibelius (*From Tradition to Gospel*) assumes that the Christian cultus was the main factor in the formulation of the record. A. F. Loisy (*Les mystères paiens et le mystère chrétien*) would deduce everything from religious ceremony.

volved everything. The service offered to Christ within his community meant the whole of life.

It is nevertheless true that the brotherhood found its centre in the common meeting, in which the believers were conscious of that fellowship with Christ which bound them together. This meeting for worship was the most powerful single factor in the moulding of Christian ideas, institutions, and literature, and against this background the history of the Gospel tradition has to be understood. The practice of reading was confined, in ancient times, to a small educated class. It was probably more widely diffused in Palestine than elsewhere, since religion was inseparable from the study of a book, and every synagogue had its school, in which children were taught to read. Yet books were scarce and expensive, and could not be the private possession of any but the few. Knowledge had to be taken in by the ear, and if Christians were to learn the record of Jesus they needed to listen to it at the church meeting. The manner in which it was there delivered would in great measure determine its character.

In our earliest glimpses of the disciples after Jesus' death we find them gathered together for worship; and the common meeting continued, and has done so to this day, to be the outstanding fact in the new religion. Its procedure was inevitably modelled on that of the synagogue—the only type of religious meeting with which the brethren were acquainted. Praise was offered to God in prayer and song. A passage was read from scripture, and was selected as bearing, in some manner, on the nature and work of Christ. An address was given in which the implications of the scripture passage were expounded. But while the synagogue service was followed, new elements were introduced which had sprung out of Christianity itself, and in Paul's Epistles we have frequent reference to these distinctive Christian additions. Paul, to be sure, speaks of the service in Gentile churches, which may have differed in some respects from that followed in Palestine; but he indicates that the practice of the mother church was normative for all others.[6] This might have been inferred without any express statement, for religious bodies are always conservative in their forms of worship. Paul tells us that place was given in the service to the utterances of "prophets," who spoke of the future and the unseen world under the impulse of the Spirit. He tells us also that in Christian worship the individual members were given opportunity for self-expression. "When ye come together, every one of you hath a psalm, hath a doctrine, hath a tongue, hath a revelation, hath an interpretation" (I Cor. 14:26). Each member was expected to contribute something of his own to the common worship. This aspect of the primitive service must never be left out of account. It belonged to the very essence of the new religion that it broke with the old conception of God as caring only for the tribe and city, or for humanity in the mass. Men had access to him now as individuals, and this must be acknowledged in the forms of worship. The expression of a communal faith

[6]Cf. Gal. 1:7–9; I Cor. 11:16; Rom. 15:27.

was combined with free utterance for the individual. Paul, indeed, finds it necessary to warn his converts against the abuse of this liberty. In a company where each man was conscious of his own religious worth all were anxious to assert themselves, and too often there was no order or dignity in the service. These conditions of license would be accentuated in a Greek community like that of Corinth, but they were inherent in the nature of the early church.

The record, then, was handed down through the meeting for common worship. We are not to conceive of the makers of the Gospels as travelling over the country and interviewing one person and another who was known to have seen Jesus or to have learned something about him from private sources. All that was necessary was to collect the accounts which were already public property through their use in the church meeting. At a later time the Gospels were themselves part of scripture, and were read out as a matter of course by way of lesson. In the early days the only Bible of the church was the Old Testament. How was it that the record of Jesus found a place in the service and thus made itself familiar?

According to one modern theory it was preserved almost accidentally by means of the address which was regularly given.[7] Some teacher spoke to the people on

---

[7] M. Dibelius (*From Tradition to Gospel*, 25 f.) supports this view from examples of Apostolic preaching in the book of Acts. He suggests that in these brief reports the original stories have been cut down to bare allusions. It might rather be inferred that a mere reference was sufficient, since the full narrative was already known.

the subject of Christian faith or duty, and would illustrate his thought by some word of Jesus, or the account of something that Jesus had done. These anecdotes would be remembered when the homily was forgotten, and would pass into general currency. Collections of them would gradually be formed, and out of this material the Gospels were eventually put together. But it is not credible that the tradition came into being in this casual fashion. We know that the Lord's sayings and example were authoritative for the church. They are so regarded by Paul, whose attitude, we may be sure, was that of all Christians. Is it conceivable that memories of Jesus were not preserved for their own sake, but only survived because they happened to be used now and then by preachers as illustrations? A theory so absurd on the very face of it ought never to have found its way into serious criticism.

A more plausible conjecture is that which would connect the tradition, at least in some of its elements, with that exercise of spiritual gifts which was part of the church service.[8] These gifts, as we know from Paul, were largely practised in the Gentile churches, and especially in that of Corinth; but there can be little doubt that they had a place in Christian worship from the earliest days. Peter declares at Pentecost that with the coming of the Spirit the words of Joel are fulfilled: "Your sons and your daughters shall prophesy." We hear of Agabus and the daughters of Philip, and of prophets who went from Jerusalem to Antioch. "Proph-

[8] A great deal is made of this in Couchod, *Le mystère de Jésus*. For a full reply, see M. Goguel, *Jesus the Nazarene*, 267 f. (Eng. Trans.).

ets and teachers" are mentioned together in an early notice which is certainly authentic (Acts 13:1). The teacher, whenever he passed from the calm exposition of truth and broke into glowing eloquence (as Paul does in some of his great passages), became a prophet.

The question arises, then, whether the prophetic element in Christian teaching may not have affected the Gospel tradition. It would happen sometimes that the teacher, caught up in the prophetic rapture, would declare that he saw Jesus perform some act or heard him speaking. These visionary experiences would be understood literally and would be incorporated into the record of Jesus' actual life. A great deal, therefore, which has come down to us as Gospel history, and perhaps most of it, may have no other origin than the rhapsody of prophets in the primitive church.

This view must not hastily be put aside, for it serves to remind us of one fact which must never be overlooked—that the early church was enthusiastic. The followers of Jesus were intensely convinced that he was still living, and doing mighty works, and speaking to his people. In this atmosphere of faith in the living Lord the record of his earthly career was moulded; and it is more than likely that in some degree the memories of Jesus have blended with that knowledge of him which came through prophetic vision. A hint of this kind may be conveyed in the story of the Transfiguration, which is described by Luke as partly an actual event and partly a dream-experience. Not infrequently, perhaps, the disciples in later days were uncertain (as all of us sometimes are) whether the thing they seemed to remember was a fact or a vision.

Yet this exercise of the spiritual gifts, though here and there it may have had some influence on the record, cannot have produced or even seriously modified it. This is apparent, for one thing, from the intrinsic character of the things recorded. Very few of them are of the kind that would suggest themselves in prophetic rapture. Nothing impresses us more in the life of Jesus, as we know it from the Gospels, than his tranquillity—his perfect clarity of thought and judgment. He breathes on the higher level as in his natural air. His greatest sayings do not come from him, like the outbursts of Paul, in sudden gusts of inspiration. Nothing, indeed, could be more alien to the Sermon on the Mount or the Parables than that ecstatic mood in which the prophets declared their visions.

Apart from the character of the records themselves we have good evidence that the memories of Jesus were not confused with the spiritual intimations. Although prophets and teachers are often mentioned together, the difference between them was recognised, and there would be no one in the primitive church who could not tell at once when the one function gave way to the other. If prophetic visions were accepted into the record, this would be done consciously and deliberately. Paul was himself a visionary, and believed that his spiritual knowledge of Christ was fully valid; yet he draws a clear distinction between that which has come to him from the Spirit and that which he has received. When he quotes a definite saying of Jesus he is careful to put in "not I but the Lord." When he can adduce no such saying he frankly admits that he has no clear word to guide him (I Cor. 7:10, 12). We need not doubt that the primitive teachers would likewise separate the knowledge given them by the Spirit from the actual tradition.

This, indeed, was possibly the very reason why the record was set apart and transmitted. If we can now see the danger that vision might be confused with facts, this would be still more apparent to the early believers. They were accustomed at every meeting to hear prophets speaking in the name of Jesus and knew how easily these deliverances might be taken for his genuine words. No restraint must be placed on the work of the Spirit, but there must be no intrusion of the spiritual revelation into the facts. There was certainly no Christian teacher who was more spiritually gifted than Paul, or who set a higher value on what he learned through the Spirit. He believed that his own knowledge of Christ, though it had come to him by vision, was no less valid than that of the immediate disciples. Yet he falls back on their evidence for the primary facts that Christ had lived with men, that he had died on the Cross, that he had risen from the dead. Apart from those historical facts there was no gospel; and they could only be established on the evidence of the original witnesses. Visions and revelations could afford no ultimate ground for faith. This was the position of Paul, and it was shared, we may be sure, by the whole early church. A line was drawn from the first between the interpretations given by the

Spirit and the fundamental facts—the tradition which had been "received from the Lord Jesus."

We must therefore look to another part of the church service as the medium through which the acts of Jesus were made known to the early worshippers. In the Christian assembly, as in the synagogue, a passage was read from scripture; and there is reason to believe that this reading was followed by some utterance of Jesus, or by some episode from his life, which served to illuminate or supplement the scriptural passage. One of the characteristics of our Gospels, and especially of the Gospel of Matthew, is the conjunction of an act of Jesus with a text of scripture which it is described as fulfilling. It may be conjectured that this practice goes back to that which had always been observed, with the difference that while Matthew quotes the relevant scripture at the close of an incident it would come at the beginning in the church service. A passage was selected from the Psalms or the Prophets in which the coming of the Messiah appeared to be foretold. This would be followed by the recounting of something in the life of Jesus which gave fulfilment to the prophecy and thus proved that he was indeed the Messiah. In his account of Jesus' own address in the synagogue at Nazareth, Luke may have in mind this custom which all his readers would recognise. He tells how Jesus read a passage from Isaiah, and then laid aside the roll and proceeded, "This day you see this Scripture fulfilled" (Lk. 4: 20, 21). In like manner the Christian teacher would follow up his read-

ing with the account of how the scripture forecast had
been realised in some event of the life of Jesus. Perhaps he would add his own comment on the story he
told, and point its bearing on Christian duty or doctrine. But the record of what the Lord had done would
stand by itself, as the essential part of the instruction
conveyed.

The handing down of the tradition would thus have
its stated place in the church service; but we must also
bear in mind the part which was taken, according to
Paul's testimony, by individual worshippers. Each member was expected to make some contribution of his own
(I Cor. 14:26); and in the early days there would
usually be some one present who had listened to Jesus.
Even at a later date there would be those who had heard
reports of him from immediate witnesses. No "psalm
or tongue or interpretation" would be so welcome as
some new anecdote of Jesus, or some saying of his which
was not yet generally known. Many of those memories
would be doubtful, or perhaps trivial and pointless.
Others would be valuable, but would seem to have little
relevance to the needs of the church, and would fall out
of sight. Now and then there would be some new reminiscence which would take its place at once in the permanent record.

In all these ways we can see how a set tradition would
form itself through the agency of the church meeting.
We can see, too, how the message and the tradition went
hand in hand. The chief purpose of the meeting was to
enforce the Christian message and apply it to the life

and needs of the community; but the message was one with the history. It could not be apprehended and explained except through the constant repetition of those deeds and words of Jesus in which the will of God had been revealed.

We have now to ask ourselves how this transmission of the record through the church meeting would affect its nature and validity. Several conclusions at once suggest themselves.

(1) It is apparent, in the first place, that a method was provided by which the tradition could be preserved, even though it was not yet committed to writing. If it had remained in the keeping of private persons, its fortune would have been highly precarious. Every one knows how the memory even of one's own actions and experiences gradually becomes uncertain. When it is passed on to another it becomes distorted, and at the third remove can hardly be recognised. Doubts as to the historical character of the Gospels are chiefly based on the assumption that they are made up of private reminiscences; and if this were their origin we should have good reason to question them. Even Peter in his later days would only have blurred impressions of things he had himself witnessed, and when Peter's story was recalled by some one else, years afterwards, very little of it would be left. But we are to conceive of the church's record as in some sense officially preserved. It belonged to the public worship and was treasured as a common possession. Changes might creep into it, as into hymns and liturgies which are subject to constant repetition;

but in the main the frequency with which it was recited would make for stability. Peter, recalling after twenty years an incident in which he had himself borne a part, would be a less trustworthy witness than a church community in which the incident had been continually retold.

(2) Again, the use of the record in the public meeting would ensure accuracy. It is often assumed that a tradition which was common property would soon lose all definite outline, like a book of reference which is handled by so many people that before long it falls to pieces. An analogy of this kind seems to be in the minds of those critics who hold that since the record was transmitted through the community we must allow for a wear and tear which battered it out of all shape. But it is evident, on a little reflection, that the parallel is misleading. A tradition adopted by the community would be safe-guarded, as it could not have been if it had been handed down through a chain of individuals, however conscientious. When you tell a story to a single auditor you can make free to modify it. Each time you tell it you may omit or add, and in this new shape the story will be accepted. But if you repeat it in a company of people, some of whom have heard it previously, you need to be careful. If you deviate at any point from the known version there is sure to be some one who will put you right. Nothing is more remarkable than the fixity of those popular tales which, in all countries, have come down by word of mouth for centuries together. They have remained the same, even in the smallest de-

tails, for the simple reason that they were known to everybody and no one was at liberty to change them. Of this we have a conspicuous instance in the Greek tragedies, which drew their subjects from the old legends. The poet had no choice but to bring in the familiar characters and incidents, for the whole audience knew the tale and insisted that it should be told in the expected way. An interesting modern instance has been brought to light by the explorer Stefansson. He tells that among the stories constantly repeated in one of the Esquimaux tribes is that of Sir John Franklin's expedition. It has come down by word of mouth from Franklin's native guides, and is told at great length, with much circumstantial detail; and at every point where it can be checked it is true to fact. The Gospel narratives, told and re-told in the church meeting, would be protected in the same manner. By frequent handling on the part of numbers of people they would not be worn down or defaced. On the contrary, each member of the community could be relied on to preserve, in its integrity, the communal possession.

(3) Again, their use in the common meeting would determine the selection of the records. It would very soon be discovered that some episodes in the life of Jesus had a more general appeal than others, and that some of the sayings impressed themselves with peculiar power. There would be problems, too, which were always recurring in the life of the church, and which called for repeated citation of particular parts of the teaching. It is significant, for instance, that so large a

place is given in our Gospels to the question of divorce, to the settlement of quarrels, to the treatment of false and unworthy brethren. The church would constantly be required to give its judgment in such matters, and on each occasion would remind itself of the demands of Jesus. There is no reason to assume that since passages in the Gospels are apposite to given situations in the early church they must have been devised for that end. They can be sufficiently explained by a process of natural selection. In its perplexities the church fell back (as it has always been doing since) on those directions of Jesus which appeared most applicable to the matter in hand. It must be noted, moreover, that the directions for the most part are general in their nature. If the church was inventing it would have taken care to put into the mouth of Jesus something that bore definitely on the particular case. It contents itself, however, with his statement of broad principles which are capable of a thousand applications. Limited, apparently, to actual sayings of Jesus, it took from them what came nearest to its purpose.

(4) Since they were connected with the worship of the church, the records must have answered some religious need. The object of the service was to confirm the faith of believers, and the life of Jesus was recalled, not so much for its intrinsic beauty and interest, as because it gave meaning to the message of salvation. It was apparent from the actions of Jesus that he was indeed Messiah, that he was endowed with divine power, that he was filled with compassion for men, and brought

healing and forgiveness. As we listen to them still in Christian worship the Gospels convey a present message—suggesting to us from all that he did in his lifetime that Jesus is still the Friend and Master and Saviour. They had a like significance to the early disciples, who were confident that he had risen from the dead and was still near to them. From the story of his life they sought the assurance that in all danger and trouble they could look for his help. This devotional interest pervades our Gospels, and explains in large measure why they have taken their present form. Everything included in them was meant, in some way, to serve the needs of a worshipping community. Here again it must be borne in mind that for the early church everything fell within the sphere of religion. A great part of the teaching is to our minds of a purely ethical nature, and many people in their study of the Synoptic Gospels are conscious of a certain disappointment, since they find so little of that element which is usually called "spiritual." But to the early church, for which Christianity in all its requirements was the new way of life, there was nothing in the Gospels which was not religion. What men ultimately sought, as they listened to these records, was fellowship with God.

(5) In the effort to adapt the tradition to use in the public meeting, a certain form would need to be imposed on it. At the outset it was probably conveyed in ordinary conversational language, but it could not be recited again and again before a worshipping assembly unless it was invested with a proper dignity. All the

more if the account of Jesus was conjoined with the scripture reading, it would acquire a form which was not too glaringly in contrast with that of the passage read. The question of form in the Gospel record has of late years assumed great importance, and will call for special consideration in a subsequent chapter. At present it is enough to note that the association of the record with the church meeting must, in some degree, have affected the form in which it was presented. Worship, by its very nature, demands a certain elevation above the ordinary modes of speech and action. Not only prayer and praise but everything that concerns the approach to God tends to take on a liturgical character.

The church service, then, was a determining factor in the moulding of the tradition. This does not imply that Christians revived their memories of Jesus only at the weekly meeting, so that nothing survived except the communal records. In the earliest years the doings of Jesus must have formed the constant subject of discussion among his followers. The story of the travellers to Emmaus, recalling their memories as they went on their journey, is doubtless taken from life. From the outset, too, instruction was one of the chief functions in the church's activity. Luke tells that the brethren at Jerusalem "attended continually to the Apostles' teaching," and this would include as its chief element the witness to Jesus. At a later time a course of instruction in Christian principles was the stated preparation for baptism, and it was so obviously necessary that it must have been offered from the first. Apollos was full of

Christian zeal, but before he proceeded to baptism he was taken in charge by Aquila and Priscilla, "who expounded unto him the way of God more perfectly" (Acts 18:26). For that part, Luke presents his Gospel to Theophilus as a more adequate record of "the things in which thou wast instructed." This intelligent convert had already passed through the ordinary course of teaching, but was eager to have some fuller and more accurate knowledge. Luke, it will be observed, takes for granted that the instruction given to Theophilus had been on the subject of Jesus' life. So in many ways the record was passed on, and the meeting was only one of the agencies for its transmission; but it was the most important one. It acted also as a crucible for all the information that was received from other sources. The facts which were brought before the assembly would be those which had proved their value; and when a place was given them in the church's worship their preservation was ensured. It was these parts of the tradition which eventually were written down and incorporated in our Gospels. Matthew and Luke have probably included a good deal more. Luke expressly claims to have taken account of "all things"—not merely the matters which were common knowledge but others which he had learned from private sources. It is possible that these additions to his material are sometimes valuable, but for the most part they bear obvious marks of rumour and legend. They represent elements in the history which had never been stabilised by use in the church meeting.

We have to do, then, with a tradition which was

formed within the community, in connection with its worship. This must be borne in mind, for it is often assumed that the Gospels were intended for propaganda. Their testimony has been challenged on this very ground, that they were written for an outside public and would naturally present the life of Jesus in the most favourable light, and would include all kinds of doubtful material so long as it had apologetic value. For a certain type of critic the Gospels are nothing but pamphlets written in a church interest for readers who had no means of testing them. Jesus is known to us only through his own advocates, and the truth might appear quite different if we could hear the other side.

Now it may be granted that the men to whom we owe our records believed in Jesus, but they were not addressing the world at large. Nothing was further from their minds than to conduct a propaganda. They spoke to their fellow-Christians, who stood in need of no persuasion. When Mark asserts that Jesus was the Messiah, the Son of God, and supports this belief by instance of his marvellous works, his object is not to prove the Messiahship to those who have called it in question. The evangelist takes for granted that his readers, like himself, have all accepted Jesus as the Messiah, and seeks only to confirm them in their faith and make clearer to them its significance. This was the purpose of those Christian meetings in which the Gospel records were handed down. The believers in their common worship were not concerned with the doubt and opposition of the outside world. They met together in order to quicken their own faith, and to deepen their sense of brotherhood by loyalty to Jesus, the one Lord.

It is argued, however, that much in the Gospels is plainly controversial.[9] Jesus is described as debating with scribes and Pharisees. Again and again he criticises the Jewish beliefs and customs in terms which may well have a contemporary reference. In the person of its Master the church itself is replying to hostile Rabbis in the Palestine of a later day. But there is no good reason to doubt that these passages of controversy are historical, and are brought into the narrative because it could not be understood without them. Jesus had aroused an opposition so bitter that it could only be satisfied with his death; how had he brought on himself this hostility? This was the first question that would be asked by those who heard the story of the Passion, and it could only be answered by some account of the conflict with the religious leaders. To this may be added that Jesus' own teaching was not fully intelligible unless it was contrasted with that which had opposed it. The controversial sections, so far from being later intrusions into the record, are the necessary key to its meaning. It may be doubted, also, whether the debates recorded in the Gospels have any aptness to the later circumstances of the church. Christianity in Palestine continued to hold fast to the Law, and was not exposed to attacks from the side of Pharisaism. The wonder is that the church which tried to thwart Paul's mission because he broke with the Law yet preserved those say-

---

[9] The fullest and ablest treatment of the controversial elements in the Gospels will be found in M. Albertz, *Die Synopitschen Streitgespräche*.

ings of Jesus in which the legal system is implicitly condemned. In several places there is an obvious attempt to qualify them—as in the distinction between the precepts of the Pharisees and their practice (Mt. 23:2), and in the assertion that the Law, in every jot and tittle, must stand for ever. It is not in Jesus' criticism of the Pharisees but in such efforts to soften it that we may detect the hand of the later church.

If there is a contemporary debate in the Gospels it must be sought in references to opinions and practices on which the church itself was divided. In Matthew, for instance, there is a whole series of passages in which the message is addressed to the Jews, while in others it is declared to be universal. A similar cleavage is apparent in Luke, where the first two chapters with their pronounced nationalism are in strange contrast with the large humanity of the book as a whole. In all the Gospels diverging views on special questions can be distinguished; for instance, on the nature and mission of the Messiah, on the date and circumstances of the Parousia, on the legitimacy of divorce. A vital and many-sided message like that of Jesus lent itself from the first to a variety of interpretation, and we have to allow for the reflection in our record of the opinions of different teachers. To this extent the Gospels betray the influence of later controversy, but it was controversy within the church. There is no evidence that anything was altered for the sake of propaganda, or under external pressure. The tradition was framed by the church, in the interest of the church itself.

CHAPTER IV

THE TRADITION AND THE COMMUNITY

THE instinct of a community has always been conservative. A number of persons are devoted to some principle or idea and are anxious to secure its permanence. Since their individual lives are brief and uncertain, they unite themselves together. It is often complained that societies of all kinds are slow to move, and foster a conventional type of thought and behaviour. This, however, is the very reason why they exist. They are formed in order to give stability to an interest which is worth preserving, and in so far as it changes they have failed in their purpose.

According to a wide-spread modern theory the primitive church was different in this respect from all other associations which we know.[1] Instead of preserving the message which it took over from Jesus, it deliberately transformed the message within a single generation. He had announced the Kingdom of God and declared himself Messiah; and a community had come into being for the maintenance of his work. But although it called itself by his name, it began, almost at once, to revise his aims and teaching. It adapted his precepts to its own changing requirements, and supplemented them

[1] W. Bousset's *Kyrios Christos* is still the ablest and most elaborate statement of this position.

with new ones from time to time. As a result of this communal action the tradition was radically modified. What has come to us as the record of Jesus is nothing, for the most part, but the history of the primitive church, reflected in a mirror.

Now it is true that the Christian community, in its earliest phase, was not an organisation. It did not begin in any official manner with the drawing up of a constitution and by-laws, ensuring that it should always preserve its original character. For a long time it had no fixed order and allowed itself to be guided in all its action by the operation of the Spirit. None the less it realised from the first that it was a Society. The very name by which its members called themselves was "the brethren," and one of the chief objects which they set before them was to strengthen in every possible way the feeling of brotherhood. If this unanimity was to be attained the first thing necessary was to make sure of the common basis. The new society existed in order to bear witness to Jesus, and there needed to be a clear conception of what he had been, and what he had done and taught. Paul acknowledges this when he indignantly denies that he was preaching "another gospel" (Gal. 1:9). He was well aware that any attempt to change the settled tradition would destroy the church. This had become the more apparent in view of the great influx of new converts who had no direct knowledge of Jesus. Their presence, it is often assumed, must have made it impossible for the church to maintain its tradition; but an inference of this kind is unfounded. With so many alien influences at work it would become imperative to have the fundamental facts of the message clearly understood and defined. If the church was not to be swept away it must anchor itself more firmly than ever to its first principles. The change in the composition of the church did not involve a change in its teaching. On the contrary, it provided the strongest motive for ensuring a firm basis.

There were special causes at work which made it easier than it might otherwise have been to guard against innovation. (1) For one thing, the primitive church was Jewish, and a reverence for tradition was ingrained in all who had undergone the Jewish discipline. The Law was a sacred possession, which was preserved with scrupulous care. Words of eminent Rabbis were handed down for generations, and were made normative for all subsequent teaching. To their new tradition the followers of Jesus would transfer that attitude of mind with which they had regarded the old. Here was something which must be treasured and revered, and passed on, in its authentic form, to the age that followed. (2) Again, the church was confined within a narrow area, and its members were all living under the same conditions. At a later time the various communities were widely scattered, and had to consult the needs of diverse races. Adaptations and changes were necessary if the mission was to make progress, although in spite of new conditions the distinctive customs and beliefs were in a wonderful degree maintained. But in Palestine itself there seem to have been few innovations, either in teaching or practice. Much has been said about the changes which must have been made in the tradition under pressure of changing circumstances. But there is no ground for supposing that the circumstances were appreciably altered. Right on to the eve of the great revolt life went on in Palestine much as it had done in the life-time of Jesus. No doubt some adptations of his teaching would be necessary, as they always are when broad principles are applied in the concrete; but there was no such change in outward conditions as would make any of the precepts out of date. (3) Again, in the Palestinian church no original teacher appeared whose ideas could in any way overshadow those of Jesus. In the Gentile church the thought of Jesus was interpreted by Paul, and afterwards by the Fourth Evangelist, with the result that Christianity developed in new directions. There was no influence in Palestine which was at all comparable with that of Paul or John. From all that we can learn of them the leaders of the mother-church were able men, but had no marked intellectual gifts. They had nothing to contribute which could be accepted even for a moment as an advance on Jesus' own teaching. So far from endeavouring to guide the church into new paths they were anxious to guard against that danger, as we can plainly see from their attitude to Paul. During its whole history the church in Palestine remained the stronghold of all the most conservative forces in the new religion, and we cannot believe that in the early days it made itself responsible for vital changes.

(4) Once more, it must never be forgotten that in the primitive church the return of Christ was expected almost immediately. All Christian thought and activity took colour from this hope, which by its nature placed an arrest on progress. If the end was to come at once there could be no object in changing anything. Paul himself, believing that the great crisis was just at hand, laid down the principle, "Let every man, in whatever position he is, therein abide with God" (I Cor. 7:24). This was certainly the mood of the church in Palestine. Its members were those who waited for the Lord's coming, and who were content, in the brief interval left to them, to remain as they were. They were in no mind to adapt the message as they had received it to the possible requirements of a future which would never come. All their desire was simply to hold fast to what they had.

There is every presumption, therefore, that the community in Palestine would preserve the Gospel tradition with little change. The attempt to make out that it was lost or perverted through the action of this community is on the face of it a hopeless one. It may indeed be granted that in all tradition, however faithfully guarded, allowance must be made for disturbing factors; and some of these are quite apparent when we examine our records of Jesus. For the early church he was the Messiah, and under the influence of this belief all his actions and the things that happened to him took on a peculiar significance. He was also "the Lord"—whom his people were sworn to obey; and from this it followed that the thought of him was intimately bound up

with the life of the brotherhood. All Christian behaviour was modelled on his example. All decisions were
made in accordance with his precepts. In every act of
worship he was believed to be present, mediating between his servants and God. It is not surprising that
the record of him came to bear the impress of the community, as a garment adapts itself to the body on which
it is constantly worn. But these factors, which have
given a certain bias to the tradition, cannot be said to
have perverted it. Through the Messianic idea the
church was enabled to see Jesus in the light that was
necessary for understanding him. There was something
in him which made men conscious that he had come
from God and was doing an inestimable work for mankind. That, as his followers realised in his life-time,
was the supreme fact about him; and the church defined
it by the Messianic idea, which was surely as appropriate as any other. Neither was the record perverted because it was interpreted through the experience of the
believers. They were striving to model themselves on
Jesus and to carry his demands into practice, and in this
effort they could not fail to see him more truly, as one
learns to understand a picture when trying to copy it.
If the language attributed to Jesus is sometimes different from what he himself could have used, it expresses
the thought in his mind. Sometimes a saying has come
down to us in several versions, and from this it has been
inferred that the words of Jesus were adapted from time
to time to new situations, and cannot now be recovered in
their original form. In a literal sense this may be true;

but those very differences in the tradition are proof of the fidelity with which the church preserved it. However it may be adapted, the saying is manifestly the same. While changing the language in order to bring out some special aspect of Jesus' meaning, the church was careful to transmit his essential thought.

It is not probable that a tradition once established in the Palestinian church would be greatly altered. The church was conservative in temper, and in its communal capacity would act as a bulwark against any wilful perversion of the record. By itself, however, this is no proof that the Gospels contain a true report of the life of Jesus. At most it can only be maintained that certain primitive beliefs were taken over by a society which was anxious to preserve them, and to hand them down in an approved form. The crucial question still remains, "How did those beliefs originate? Can we have any assurance that they correspond with a reality?" No competent scholar would now hold that they were a conscious fabrication; but there is always the possibility that they grew, pretty much of their own accord, out of materials furnished by current Judaism. Such a view might seem to be supported by the many parallels to our Gospels which can be found in the later Jewish literature. The parallels are often far-fetched; but it is undeniable that for almost every Gospel saying and incident there is some analogy in Jewish writings which still survive, and these can be only a fraction of what is lost. Is it not conceivable that out of this great mass of Jewish wisdom and legend some body of teachers selected the more valuable elements, and formed them into a new tradition, attached to the name of Jesus? The sect which adopted this tradition may have guarded it faithfully, but this does not make history out of a structure which, from the outset, was artificial. A theory of this kind has frequently been put forward with various modifications,[2] but it does not carry us far. That some Rabbinical sayings have been attributed to Jesus is not unlikely, and he himself may have made use occasionally of the maxims of previous teachers. When a thought had already been expressed as well as it needed to be, he saw no object in saying it differently. But to explain the whole of Jesus' teaching as a tissue of Rabbinical maxims, carefully selected and interwoven, is to evade the real problem. For one thing, the sifting out of those vital elements from the vast accumulation of Jewish legalism would have been a task of infinite labour, and would have called for a spiritual discernment hardly inferior to that which produced them. Moreover, when we compare the sayings of Jesus with their Jewish parallels we find invariably that something is added which makes all the difference. Even when they seem to be identical, they are brought into a new context—they are subordinated to a new conception of God and of man's relation to him. It is in this new factor that Christianity consists. We cannot but feel that a creative power has been at work, putting the breath of life into everything that has been borrowed. The play of *Macbeth* is

[2] *Cf.* the discussions in Vol. I of F. J. Foakes Jackson and K. Lake, *The Beginnings of Christianity*.

not explained when we have discovered in a forgotten chronicle the materials which went to the making of it. Something has been taken from what existed already, but just as evidently something has been given; and the real question has not even been touched until we consider what it was. This is no less true of our Gospels.

It must be admitted, therefore, that every theory of the tradition as devised, in some manner, by the primitive church, is beset with difficulties. The most natural assumption will always be that Jesus lived the life and spoke the words ascribed to him, and that the part of the church was that of transmitting an authentic record. This, however, is only a negative conclusion, forced on us by the improbability of any other view. Are there any positive grounds for believing that the tradition is authentic? Does it contain within itself the convincing evidence that it was not made by the church, but goes back to historical facts? This must always be the ultimate problem of Gospel criticism.

It is a problem to which no definite solution is possible. All historical facts must be accepted on testimony, and there is no testimony which may not be questioned. An able advocate can make out, in the face of a dozen good witnesses, that the events on which judgment must be passed did not happen. With the Gospel narratives we have the further difficulty that they stand alone, and cannot be compared with other testimonies by which their truth might in some measure be established. The nearest approach to such independent witness is to be found in the references of Paul, which are, indeed, of inestimable value. They prove to us, on the word of a contemporary, that Jesus lived, and had won such devotion from his followers that they regarded him as Messiah. They tell us of certain facts which had come to Paul's knowledge from companions of Jesus whom he had personally known. Paul, however, was concerned with the message rather than with the life. He had resolved to know nothing of Christ after the flesh, and only touches incidentally on the history. In any case it may be argued that Paul was himself a child of the primitive church. His Epistles come to us from a time when the primary Gospel literature was taking shape, and are open to the same suspicions. There is no first-hand evidence by which we can test our records; and if there were it would probably help us little, for the question of credibility would only face us again in some new form. Those who demand that our accounts of Jesus should be linked directly with indubitable fact are asking for the impossible. We reach a point here, as in all historical evidence, when we must rest everything on some one's bare word.

Yet there are solid grounds for the conviction that what the church preserved was the record of an actual history. For one thing, as has been pointed out already, the church itself has to be explained. It is easy to say that the Gospels were produced by the Christian community; but what was the community? It consisted of men and women who acknowledged Jesus to be the Messiah, and from this it is certain that Jesus had existed, and had acted in such a manner as to awaken faith and devotion. The very fact of the church involves the reality of the life—just as a building which rests apparently on a sheet of water is proof that it has a rock beneath it. In like manner, the church's message needs to be accounted for. There can be no question that the church proclaimed a message which was carried to all nations, and it is contended that this message gave birth to a tradition. But how had the message itself originated? It cannot have developed out of Judaism, for at all essential points it broke away from the religion of the Law. Faith took the place of legal observance. Righteousness was identified with the new will. The promise made to Israel was extended to all races of men. The Messianic hope was associated with the Cross. In this new religion the pious Jew could see nothing but a betrayal of all that was most sacred in his beliefs, and his attitude to it was that of Paul the persecutor. How could a message so abhorrent to all Jewish sentiment have emerged from Judaism? It can only have done so because something had happened which had revolutionised the old conceptions. When a mountain is rent by a deep chasm, we know that at some time there has been an earthquake. When Judaism is found in one particular age to change into something different, there can be no talk of development. A convulsion has taken place, due to some quite specific cause; and the only cause which can be deemed at all adequate is of the kind known to us through the Gospel history.

This conclusion is now accepted, in however grudging a fashion, by all serious students of Christian origins. Even those who cannot believe in the history are driven to postulate something which took the place of it. They assume that Jewish religion had come in contact with some other; that certain elements in it which had hitherto lain separate had suddenly fused together; that a forgotten myth or speculation had forced its way upward from subterranean depths. Behind this message which came to light in the first century and produced the Christian church, there must have been some extraordinary event in man's outward or spiritual life: that is now admitted by all. And the one event which will explain everything is the emergence of a great personality, such as is described in our Gospels. The church and the message both arose out of that historical life which had preceded them. This is the conclusion which cannot be avoided, and there are several considerations which appear to make it certain.

(1) We cannot but perceive, for one thing, that the record does not properly answer its purpose. It was meant to confirm the church in its belief that Jesus was the Messiah, who had fulfilled the hope of Israel and had brought life and salvation to the world. But if the church had itself devised a mythical history to suit its purpose, it performed its work with a singular lack of skill. It was free, according to the hypothesis, to put anything it pleased into the life of Jesus, and so construct the sort of history it needed. What it has given us is the story of a teacher who had worked obscurely in a remote province, who had roused against him pow-

erful enemies and was compelled in the end to yield to them, who was accepted by men as one of themselves and who did little, to all outward seeming, that was not within the range of normal human life. Here and there, to be sure, we meet with a surprising miracle, or with an incident like the Transfiguration; but these episodes at once strike us as doubtful. They are out of keeping with the prevailing tone of the narrative, and we feel justified in supposing that whatever core of fact may be in them has been elaborated and overlaid by the later reflection of the church. If the history had been made to order, for the confirmation of Christian belief, every-thing would have been of this character. As it is, the most uncritical reader is at once aware when myth or doctrine has encroached on the history. It cannot be said that the Gospel writers have been wholly success-ful even in their effort to prove the Messiahship of Jesus. Mark has plainly made it his object to adduce evidence for this belief, and on this ground it has been argued that his work cannot be regarded as historical. The author must be either inventing his facts or modi-fying them in the interest of a doctrine. But to this it may be answered that if his one purpose is theological he has woefully failed in it. The facts which he brings forward do not prove, except to those who are convinced already, that Jesus was "the Messiah, the Son of God." Those acts of power, of which so much is made, might have been done by any wonder-worker, or might be ac-counted for by natural causes. Those prophecies which Jesus is said to have fulfilled have little real bearing on the incidents with which they are connected. It is admitted by Mark himself that the Pharisees were dissatisfied with the "signs" which Jesus offered, and asked him for a clear and decisive one, which he refused. The church was much more anxious than the Pharisees for an unanswerable sign, and a fictitious narrative could have supplied it without difficulty; but Mark is obviously limited to the given facts, and has to make the best of them. In like manner the account of the Last Supper does not express the sacramental ideas which the church would fain have read into it; the parable of the sower does not apply to the later mission, as Mark has tried to make it. All the evangelists are constantly seeking, as he does, to fit the later ideas into the history, but their effort is rarely successful. The record and the doctrine, as soon as we look even a little way beneath the surface, are incompatible. This, perhaps, was one reason why Paul made so little of the Gospel tradition. That he was well acquainted with it cannot be doubted, but he was conscious that it did not bear out his theology; and the teaching of Paul was not essentially different from that of the Palestinian church.[3]

The evangelists, then, have failed to disguise the cleavage between the tradition and the later beliefs, and of this there can only be one explanation. A record had come down in the church which was known to contain the authentic memories of Jesus' life. With this record no liberties could be taken beyond a certain point. It

[3]Cf. Gal. 1:6–8. It is significant that while Paul takes issue with the mother-church on the question of the Law, he assumes that its doctrinal position is fully in harmony with his own.

was not fully consistent with the doctrines and practices which were now based on it; but as the historical record it had to be allowed to stand. The church made what it could of the facts, and strained all probabilities to suit them to its purpose, but it could do no more. Behind the accepted beliefs there was a body of historical fact out of which they had grown, but with which they could not be fully reconciled. This is perhaps our strongest proof that the tradition is rooted in an authentic history.

(2) Again, the record is composed, for the most part, of isolated incidents and sayings. The material had evidently come down in this fragmentary condition, and the chief aim of the evangelists is to combine it in an ordered whole. They repeatedly differ from each other as to the context of an anecdote or saying, and it is too often apparent that the choice has been made by guess-work. The narrators before them had evidently been faced by the same problems of arrangement, and had solved them in the same precarious fashion. This detached character of the record has been apparent ever since the critical enquiry began. The Gospels, as we now have them, have been compiled from earlier sources, and these, in turn, can be resolved into a great number of unrelated fragments.[4] From this fact alone it is possible to draw some far-reaching conclusions. If the church had itself been responsible for the record it would not have devised a series of episodes which in

---

[4]This is demonstrated in detail by K. L. Schmidt, *Der Rahmen der Geschichte Jesu.*

themselves are frequently obscure and unintelligible. No conceivable object could be served by the invention of stray passages of which no one could see the application. Take, for instance, the saying "Agree with thine adversary quickly while thou art in the way with him, etc." (Mt. 5:25)—which as we now have it is a mere piece of prudential wisdom, hardly to be deemed worthy of preservation. It must have formed part of a parable, or was intended in some figurative sense which the context would have made clear; but with its isolation the key to its meaning has been lost. This passage is only one of a large number which cannot be accounted for except on one hypothesis. Included in the tradition there were sayings, parables, incidents which were no longer understood. Their survival was due to some accident, or to some trick of memory which had left out the thing of most importance, so that now they stand up like pillars after the roof they once supported has fallen in. If the church continued to treasure them it must have been because they were part of the genuine record of Jesus; no other reason can be conceived.

(3) Again, there is hardly anything in the Gospels which does not find its most natural explanation in the circumstances of Jesus' own life. According to modern theory it was the community which framed the tradition, ascribing to Jesus, whenever the need arose, some action or precept by which it might be guided. Either it invented some occasion in his life when he was called on to deal with the given problem, or it laid hold of some vague reminiscence and worked it up into an anec-

dote which furnished the required moral. On this view the task of criticism is to determinate the "living situation,"—the connection with early church history, in which each passage in the Gospels had its origin.[5] For example, there was the case of the wealthy man who sincerely wished to join the Christian fellowship, but still hankered after his possessions. The question of how to deal with such converts must have come up many times in the primitive church, which aimed at practising, at least in some degree, a community of goods. So the story was devised of how Jesus was once met with this very problem, and gave his judgment. With a little ingenuity it is not difficult to place most of the Gospel incidents in such "living situations"; but there is no need for so explaining them. The story of the rich young ruler, taken just as it stands, is natural and touching and beautiful. The new version of it is forced and pedantic, and also misses the point—which is that there can be no discipleship without renunciation: the question of whether rich men should be admitted to the church is entirely a side-issue. Moreover there are many episodes in the Gospels which cannot, even by straining, be fitted into any church situation—the scenes in the synagogue at Capernaum, the healing of the centurion's servant and of the woman who touched Jesus in the crowd, the stories of Zacchæus and the penitent woman and the paralytic who was let down through the roof. The sayings, more particularly, cannot have been in-

[5]It is unfortunate that most of the exponents of Form Criticism have so deeply committed themselves to this theory of the "Sitz im Leben."

tended to meet the definite exigencies which arose in the early church. They were applicable, no doubt, to those occasions, just as they have been ever since to the needs and questionings of men in all manner of circumstances. Their greatness consists in nothing else than this universality. They have to be interpreted not from their aptness to the difficulties of the church in Palestine but from their profound relation to the permanent facts of human life. If the church had wished to invent something which would give explicit direction for its special needs, it would not have been content with those broad statements of duty. It required sayings of which the bearing was unmistakable, and these would have been just as easy to invent as the others—indeed infinitely easier.

Nothing, in fact, could be less justified than the claim that by connecting a Gospel episode with a supposed church problem we put it back into its "living situation"—into the soil out of which it grew. This attempt to re-plant turns out, in almost every instance, to be an uprooting. The passage refuses to unfold itself in its full wealth of meaning unless it is related to the life of Jesus—to the whole of his thought and character. That is its native soil, the necessary texture from which it cannot be severed. The community indeed availed itself of what Jesus had taught, by word and example, and applied this teaching to its own needs. To this extent the history as we have it was affected by the experiences of the early church. But the connection of Jesus' teaching with his own life and purpose was never forgotten.

Along with the flower the church retained the roots, with some of the soil still clinging to them. The precepts of Jesus could not be separated from his living example, and that is the very reason why our Gospels came to be written.

(4) Again, the modification of incidents and sayings in view of later conditions is itself a proof that they go back to something authentic. As a rule the contrary inference is drawn. When we find, for instance, that the teaching on divorce is given differently in the several Gospels, or that the command to forgive the erring brother becomes in Matthew a formal rule for church discipline, must we not assume that Jesus left no directions, and that the community itself devised a mode of procedure which it altered from time to time? This, however, is to ignore a principle which holds good in all historical enquiry. It happens invariably that the same fact is reported in varying terms by the several authorities, each of them with a bias of his own. But the historian does not on this account question the fact. On the contrary he knows that something of the kind must have happened, or there would have been no need for explaining it from all those different points of view. His task is to compare the conflicting reports and discover the truth which gave rise to all of them and perhaps is disclosed in none. This principle holds good with regard to the Gospel records. They are frequently at variance, and the effort to make a special application of something done or said by Jesus may be obvious. This, however, does not mean that all the accounts may

be set aside. It proves, rather, that we have to do with a genuine tradition, for if there had been no fact there would have been no dissension.

(5) This brings us to another, and in some respects the most convincing evidence that the church transmitted an authentic history. Ever and again in the Gospels we meet with sayings which were opposed to later practice, or which had ceased to be understood. Reference has been made already to the prominence given to Jesus' criticism of the legal system. The church in Palestine was faithful to the Law, and upheld it against the innovations of Paul. If it preserved a strain in Jesus' teaching which was so inconsistent with its own position, this can only have been because Jesus had thus spoken. So with the admissions of blindness and weakness on the part of the disciples, who for the church were consecrated figures, and the account of how Jesus' brethren, now pillars of the church, had sought to withdraw him from his work. Very significant, too, is the absence of all teaching on Baptism, the complete silence on the work of the holy Spirit, the primary place assigned to the message of the Kingdom, which for the later church had ceased to constitute the gospel. In like manner, sayings are attributed to Jesus which were no longer intelligible to the church that transmitted them. It is evident that neither Matthew nor Luke can make anything of the words "The Kingdom of heaven is taken by violence" (Mt. 11:12; Lk. 16:16). Mark admits that the most serious testimony brought against Jesus at his trial was that he had been heard to say, "Destroy

this temple and I will re-build it in three days" (Mk. 14:58); but Mark was ignorant, as we are now, what was meant by that fateful saying. Parables of Jesus are recorded at length, but it is quite apparent that the point of not a few of them has been missed—*e.g.*, the Good Samaritan and the Labourers in the Vineyard.[6] This frequent misunderstanding on the part of the evangelists has sometimes been set down to their imperfect knowledge of the Aramaic idiom in which the records had come to them. Attempts have been made, and perhaps in some cases legitimately, to recover the true sense by re-translation.[7] But most probably the key to many of the sayings had been lost before any documents, Greek or Aramaic, had come into existence. So far from creating the record of Jesus the church was often in a difficulty as to its import. It reverently preserved the tradition as it had come down from the earliest teachers, but some things in Jesus' words and actions were enigmatic, and had probably been so from the first.

In all these ways we can discover evidence of a positive nature that the Gospel record was independent of the community by which it had been transmitted. This does not mean that the community was nothing but a neutral medium. Its influence was a powerful one, and

---

[6]B. M. T. Smith (*The Synoptic Parables*) has clearly demonstrated that the evangelists have repeatedly misunderstood the parables which they record.

[7]Dr. C. C. Torrey (*The Four Gospels* and *Our Translated Gospels*) has maintained, with immense learning and ingenuity, that the Gospels are wholly translated from Aramaic. The theory will not stand, in the face of assured critical results; but the author succeeds in showing that behind many single passages an Aramaic original can be detected.

must never be disregarded. To some extent it was exercised unconsciously, as always happens when events are narrated with a full knowledge of what has followed them. Looking back on the life of Jesus in the light of its own faith and experience the church could not but read a significance in all his action which had not been apparent at the time. He had proclaimed the Kingdom, and must therefore have foreseen all those signs of its coming which had been witnessed since; and predictions are assigned to him which he never uttered. He had given instructions to his disciples, and these are expanded, so as to bear directly on the missionary work that was now in process. He had confessed himself the Messiah, and all that had happened to him is seen, in retrospect, as evidence of his claim. Allowance must also be made for a conscious influence on the part of the community. For one thing, it deliberately selected from all that it knew about Jesus those memories which were helpful to it in its own struggle. Perhaps there is nothing in the Gospels which did not find its way there because of some need experienced by the early church. For the most part its needs were the large human ones of which all communities are conscious; but here and there we meet with passages which can be related definitely to conditions in Palestine. Besides its work of selection, the church permitted itself at some points to modify the record. It was the practice of the Rabbis to add something of their own, by way of emphasis or qualification, to the counsels they transmitted; and there is a suggestion in at least one verse in the Gospels that this example was followed by the Christian teachers. "Every scribe who is instructed towards the Kingdom of heaven [*i.e.*, every teacher of the Christian message] is like a householder who brings out of his treasure things new and old" (Mt. 13:52). His first duty is to guard the tradition, but he must also be able to interpret and apply it. There is no reason to suppose that the Christian teachers took out of their treasure new things which they had themselves put in. The changes they made were intended only to elucidate what they actually found. In passages that seem the most doubtful we can always feel that we have the import of what Jesus said, though he may not have used these literal words.

There is no ground for believing that the community, though in details it may have modified the record, in any sense produced it. The community itself is, indeed, the decisive guarantee for the record. By no accumulation of evidence can it ever be demonstrated that Jesus lived the life described in our Gospels. There is not a single episode in their record of which we can be entirely certain. Our own senses constantly deceive us, and we have no means of verifying things reported, in documents many centuries old. Yet we do know that after Jesus' death a community arose which believed in him with a boundless devotion. We know that this community had a conception of God and a moral standard and a number of practices and doctrines which distinguished it from all others. There is no source from which these things can have been borrowed, but they do correspond with that teaching which is ascribed to Jesus in the Gospels. The presumption surely is that they came from Jesus. Attention has been too much concentrated in recent years on what the church may have given, out of its own reflection and activity. This contribution of the church has been magnified until it seems to account for everything. Yet when all is said the church was the society of those who believed in Jesus, and who had been won to that belief by the knowledge of what he had been. All that the church may have given goes back, in the last resort, to what it received from Jesus himself.

It will never be possible to separate with any precision those elements in the record which are purely historical from those which were added by the community. If this could be done it would probably be found that the church was responsible for very little. From the few notices which have come to us we can gather that the Palestinian Christians were not creative. Stephen and the Hellenists, with their more liberal understanding of the message, were forced to part company with the native believers. Paul, with his splendid original genius, found no welcome in Palestine, and had to seek a new field among the Gentiles. The Christians in Palestine, although they had responded to the message of Jesus, continued in all their habits of mind to be Jews, and into their Christianity they seem to have carried their Jewish reverence for the letter. It was in virtue of this very literalism that they performed their inestimable service to the new religion. While in the Gentile world the message was transformed by a succession of great thinkers, the Palestinian teachers took their stand on the facts, which they often apprehended very imperfectly. They were content to remember what Jesus had done. They piously collected his actual words, and treasured them, as far as was possible, unaltered. Even in their Christianity they were confined within the pale of traditional religion, and for this reason we owe to them the priceless tradition of Jesus.

CHAPTER V

THE ORAL TRADITION

JESUS proclaimed his message by word of mouth, and looked forward to its diffusion by the same means. His life was cut short before he could give effect to his wider plans; but at least on one occasion he sent out his disciples to announce, as he himself had done, that the Kingdom was at hand. Mark says explicitly that he chose them in order that they might act as his "heralds," promulgating his gospel by the living voice (Mk. 3:14).

After his death we find them entering immediately on their mission, though it now consisted not merely in the announcement of the Kingdom but in the vindication of Jesus himself as the Messiah. They had no thought of anything except an oral teaching. Not only was this in accordance with Jesus' own example, but all written testimony was deemed to be superfluous since the Parousia was expected at any moment. Moreover, the field of activity was limited to Jerusalem and its neighbourhood, and the brethren were in daily intercourse with one another. The first mention we have of writing, in connection with the work of the church, is in Luke's account of the Council, when a decree was drawn up in the name of the leading Apostles (Acts 15:20). It is to be noted, however, that writing is here assumed to be the usual practice in communicating with brethren at a distance. There is no reason to doubt that the church had always numbered among its members men who were accustomed to write, and that writing was freely employed for various church purposes. The poorer members, for instance, were supported by the community, and this would entail the keeping of a roll. Meetings were held for the making of grave decisions, and there would need to be some record of these meetings. It has been observed that certain passages in the early chapters of Acts have all the appearance of extracts from official documents—minutes preserved at Jerusalem or Antioch, from which Luke obtained the most trustworthy part of his information.

The enquiry into the origins of the church has too often proceeded on the assumption that it was made up entirely of illiterate people who had to entrust everything to memory. Analogies to Christian tradition have been drawn from the rudest phases of culture—from the practice of savage tribes, of Arabian nomads, of the peasantry of the Middle Ages.[1] This is surely a strange historical error. The first century was the culminating period of ancient civilisation, and the Jews were one of the most highly civilised of ancient peoples. It may be that most of the Christian converts were "unlearned and ignorant men" (Acts 4:13), but this account of them must

---

[1] K. L. Schmidt (*Die Stellung der Evangelien in der allgemeinen Literaturgeschichte*) places the Gospel records in the class of "Kleinliteratur," *i.e.*, popular broadsides, etc., as contrasted with genuine literature. Dibelius seems to adopt a similar view—which has nothing in its favour except that the Gospel narratives are brief and simple. It seems hard to exclude them, for that reason, from the class of good writings.

be taken in a relative, one might almost say a technical sense. They did not belong to the class of professional Rabbis; but from this it did not follow that they were utterly uncultivated. Christianity at all times has made difficult demands, moral and intellectual. We should naturally expect that those who were attracted to it in the early days should have been much above the general level, and from all we can learn of them it is abundantly clear that they were. The audiences for which Paul wrote his Epistles must have had no ordinary intelligence, and this would be equally true of the Palestinian Christians. By the very fact that they had broken with conventional Judaism they gave proof that they were able to think independently. It is generally found, too, that the higher spiritual interests go together, and that the man of religious nature is also the most devoted to things of the mind. This would be true in the primitive age, as it is today. Many foolish theories which have befogged the modern enquiry would be cleared out of the way if we would only bring ourselves to realise that the early Christians were not ignorant boors, who held erratic beliefs because they knew no better. In the most real sense they were educated men. If it had been otherwise they could never have appreciated the records of Jesus and gathered them finally into books which are among the very greatest in the world's literature.

For a considerable time, however, the church did not put its tradition into writing. This is evident from the fact that the same narratives and sayings have come down to us in varying language, as they could not have done if they had been fixed from the outset in written form. But if writing was not employed the reason is by no means to be sought in illiteracy. The supposition that no one was able to write, in this highly intelligent community, dwelling in the capital of a nation which held writing in peculiar honour, is nothing else than absurd. It is in other ways that we must explain why nothing was written, even in years much later than the initial period when the Lord's return was immediately expected. Something must be attributed to the example of scribal teaching. The function of the Rabbi was to transmit by word of mouth what he had so learned from his predecessors; and the Christian teacher in Palestine would naturally follow this established practice. It is significant that when Paul speaks of "transmitting" to his converts that which he had "received" (I Cor. 15:3), he uses the identical terms which were employed in the Rabbinical schools. He takes for granted that the Christian method is the same as the Jewish. Again, for the early Christian mind the message, by its very nature, required to be spoken. It was the "kerygma," the proclamation. That term had been applied to it from the first, and had been taken over from Jesus himself, who had associated it with the spoken word. His example was binding on his disciples. In the early years, too, the effectiveness of the message depended on its coming directly by the living voice. The teacher could stand before his hearers and declare, "I myself was present when Jesus spoke this word, or did this wonderful action." A story is always more impressive when recounted by one who has participated in the event, and can vouch in his own person for the truth of it. You may have heard or read it already, but when you fall in with an eye-witness you want to hear it again from his own lips, and it seems to become quite new. Again, something must be attributed to the force of custom. In religion, more than anywhere else, rules that have been followed for some time become sacrosanct, and by their practice of oral teaching the primitive Apostles would establish a convention which it was difficult to break. Since the first days the community had been used to have the record orally delivered, and would dislike to have it fixed in writing, even when the hope of the Parousia was fading and the immediate disciples were passing from the scene. A doubt may be hazarded as to whether the Palestinian church ever possessed a written record. There are clear traces of Aramaic originals behind the Greek documents on which our Gospels were based; but it does not follow that those originals existed in a written form. The presumption is rather that the whole enterprise of writing out the tradition was carried through, from the beginning, in Greek. In this respect, as in many others, the Gentile church would seem to have departed from Palestinian custom.

We have to conceive, then, of a tradition which for some years was orally transmitted, and which consisted of detached episodes and sayings. That they were originally separate is evident from their connection in the Gospels by links which are almost always formal and artificial. ("And it came to pass." "He arose from thence." "On another day." "When he had come into the house.") When the Gospels were written these passages had to some extent been grouped together in earlier documents, but the evangelists are clearly conscious that the record before them has no inner cohesion. They feel themselves at liberty to rearrange the pieces in new settings and combinations. They treat their material as consisting of single blocks, which the builder is free to manipulate in the manner he thinks best.

In recent years an intensive study has been given to these primary elements, these ultimate cells or crystals out of which the Gospels are composed. It can hardly be doubted that they represent the tradition as it existed in the age prior to that of written documents, and by closer analysis of their nature and structure we may hope to learn more of the conditions under which the record took shape. The line of enquiry is a new one, and perhaps has awakened false expectations. It has been hailed in many quarters as at last providing a clue to all those problems of Gospel criticism which have hitherto baffled solution. This is not the fault of the theory, or of the eminent scholars who have developed it. Every new method is bound to prove disappointing. It seems at first to promise an explanation of everything, and is gradually found to lead only a little way forward.

In some respects it is unfortunate that attention has been so largely directed at the present time to the new line of approach. Whatever may have been the original sources of our Gospels there can be no doubt that the evangelists worked with written documents, the nature

lich cannot be said to have yet been fully deter-
d. It may fairly be questioned whether the oral
tradition, which is hypothetical, can be profitably discussed until we have learned more about the written
tradition, which is in our hands. A biologist, seeking
to trace out the evolution of the horse, must first examine
the animal in all its known varieties, and so work backward. He must not begin by conceiving the original
horse, and then proceed to show how it must have developed from this phase into the horse we know. Too
often this would appear to be the method now adopted
by Gospel critics. They assume the types of oral tradition current in the primitive church, and so consider
the various stages through which these types must have
passed until they resulted in the writings which we now
possess. The true method of enquiry is undoubtedly the
opposite one, from the known to the unknown.

It has to be recognised, therefore, that all theories
about the oral tradition are still tentative, and await
the fuller investigation of a number of questions re-
lating to our present Gospels. What was the nature and
extent of the document Q? Did Matthew and Luke
use it directly, or had it already been edited, and embodied in some larger work? When a saying or incident has come to us in several versions, how are we to
determine which is preferable, and how the difference
arose? To what extent do the Greek records bear evidence of translation from Aramaic? Have our evangelists simply transcribed their sources, or have they
modified them, more or less seriously, by editorial

methods? These are all questions to which a more intensive analysis of the existing Gospels may provide an answer, and until it is forthcoming no one can pass any confident judgment on the underlying tradition. The literary questions are the more urgent as the new criticism is occupied so much with the matter of "forms"; and it is precisely these which would suffer most in a process of translation and editing. A translator is more concerned with substance than with form; an editor creates new forms in which he combines those parts of his documents which he considers most valuable. It may be granted that ideas and facts have been conscientiously transferred from the earlier records to our present Gospels, but what of the forms? If they are ever in any degree to be recovered, it can only be by a literary criticism, more patient and exact than has yet been attempted.

It must be acknowledged, therefore, that all study of the oral tradition is still, for the most part, premature. For a long time to come the investigation must concern itself, as hitherto, with the Synoptic problem, which has not yet been brought within sight of a solution. At present the temptation is to take liberties with the written documents, and to force them into the shape required of them by given theories.[2] The new enquiry has to this extent been a positive obstruction to progress. A warning may here be derived from the history of Homeric criticism, with which, from the time of its

[2]M. Dibelius, *Die Botschaft von Jesus Christus, wiederhergestellt* is an attempt to reconstruct the tradition in what may have been its original form.

inception more than a century ago, the criticism of the Gospels has been curiously linked. The theory was put forward, and for some time was generally accepted, that the *Iliad* and *Odyssey* were compounded of a great number of ballads, different in date and authorship and revised by several editors. In this account of the poems there were doubtless some elements of truth; but the main effect was disastrous. Homer was sacrificed in the interests of a theory. His most splendid passages were discarded because they were too good for a primitive ballad or lengthened it out unduly. Sane critics are now agreed that if we are ever to explain these poems we must take them as they are, not as they might have been if they had been made according to our formula. It is more than likely that a similar judgment will finally be reached with regard to the Gospel tradition.

The new enquiry, however, has compelled us to give attention to the all-important fact that before it was written down the record had passed through an oral phase. Scholars had long recognised this fact, but had never properly weighed its significance. They were content to say that the tradition in its earliest form was fluid, and by making this admission they felt that they had disposed of all previous questions and could now settle down to their real task of examining the written sources. Matter, however, even in its fluid state is subject to laws which need to be ascertained. What are now the mountain ranges assumed their contour when the earth was a molten mass; and we have to transport ourselves into that remote past before we can explain the realities before our eyes. The Gospels as we have them are in written form, and the business of the scholar is with the actual writings. Yet he can make little of the later formations unless he takes account of the time when there was no writing, but only the fluid mass of the oral tradition.

It has been the signal service of the newer criticism to indicate the "forms" or patterns which are traceable throughout our Gospels.[3] Those separate passages of which the tradition originally consisted seem all to have been constructed on given models, according to the nature of their subject. Seven or eight of these "forms" have been distinguished, although none of the schemes proposed can be made to fit in exactly with the material as we now have it. Our Gospels, it must never be forgotten, are the final outcome of a long process in which the records had been edited and re-edited, and all efforts to determine their original structure must be conjectural at the best. There may have been a time when the forms were rigid, and miracle, parable, historical incident, moral maxim and anecdote, controversy and rebuke had all their set patterns, from which there could be no deviation. As it is, we can only speak of an approximation to certain types which may once have been definite but are now blurred beyond all hope of restoration.

---

[3]The main forms distinguished are: (1) miracle stories; (2) "paradigms" or "pronouncement stories"; (3) aphorisms; (4) tales; (5) legends; (6) controversies; (7) apocalyptic utterances. Each writer, however, has his own classification, and the effort to multiply and isolate the patterns has tended to discredit a method which in principle is sound.

The main contention, however, appears to be a sound one that the tradition, in its oral phase, consisted of a large number of detached pieces, each of which was cast in something like a regular mould. Even now the forms can be made out, at least in outline, like the first tracing under a picture which has been altered and elaborated. Perhaps the most frequent and the best defined of these forms is the illustrative anecdote, in which a weighty saying of Jesus is appended to an incident in his life. He passed, for instance, through the fields with his disciples on a Sabbath day, and they began to pluck ears of corn. The Pharisees objected to this breach of the Law, and he said, "The Sabbath was made for man, not man for the Sabbath" (Mk. 2:27). Or he was at supper, and publicans and sinners were eating with him. His enemies criticised his action and he said, "They that are whole have no need of the physician; I came to call not righteous men but sinners (Mk. 2:17). Children were brought to him for his blessing, and the disciples drove them off. He was displeased and called the children to him and said, "Of such is the Kingdom of heaven" (Mt. 19:14). The Gospels are full of such anecdotes, and it is obvious that they are all told in much the same way. Jesus does something, objection is taken, he justifies himself by a saying of far-reaching import. Or some one comes to him with a question, representing the point of view which has hitherto been accepted. He answers with another question, suggesting a deeper truth. In all these anecdotes the important thing is not the incident itself but the comment of Jesus which it called forth.

The thing that happened is only the framework for the saying.

The miracle stories form a considerable part of all the Gospels; and they too are recounted according to a scheme which may be called conventional. Some one comes to be healed, the gravity of his affliction is emphasised, the onlookers are incredulous of Jesus' power, yet he performs the miracle and its efficacy is made apparent in some striking way. In like manner a plan may be discerned in the controversial passages of the narrative. A commonly accepted belief is stated, usually by a scribe or Pharisee, and is supported by a text of scripture. Jesus refutes it, also in the light of scripture, and adds his rebuke to those who have misconstrued the will of God.

One thing is at once apparent when these "forms" are examined. On the face of them they are artificial. Things do not happen in real life according to a uniform plan, and we cannot believe that Jesus was always encountering incidents which lent themselves exactly to pointed sayings, which he was able on every occasion to produce instantly. There has clearly been some manipulation of the facts in order to enforce their significance. The hand of the narrator has been at work, giving a turn in some required direction to the action of Jesus. This criticism, however, must not be pushed too far. Though we may call it artificial the form is natural, and one may almost say inevitable. In the report of any memorable saying a method similar to that of the Gospels has always to be followed—a note of the occasion, a remark or question, the unanswerable reply. The biography of any famous man affords many analogies—not to speak of the variety column in any newspaper. It may be true that in real life things do not happen in just that way, but the art of the narrator consists in leaving out irrelevant details and sharpening the point. No reasonable person would complain that truth has been sacrificed, for the effort has been to bring out the truth more clearly. So also the form adopted in the miracle stories is entirely natural. We still follow it instinctively in describing anything remarkable that has come under our observation. The hearer must be made to feel that the incident was out of the common, that no one believed it could happen, that it did happen beyond the possibility of doubt. It is difficult to understand the argument, sometimes advanced quite gravely, that the Gospel stories are open to suspicion because they are couched in particular forms. The same argument might be urged against almost any narrative. In every age there are recognised modes of telling a story, and if we want information about things which then happened we must be willing to receive it in that manner. The mere fact that forms are employed in the recording of the Gospel tradition has no bearing whatever on its substance.

One thing must never be forgotten. From the outset a peculiar significance would attach itself, in the minds of all Christians, to the things done by Jesus. Stories told of him would be something more than interesting

anecdotes. Things said by him were no mere epigrams
or sage reflections, like those ascribed to celebrated Rabbis. Behind all the record lies the conviction that Jesus
was the Messiah, who spoke with a divine authority.
There is a constant suggestion that he was a being of
superior order, and that his sayings were of the nature
of oracles, beyond which there was no appeal. This
conception of the unique dignity of Jesus reflects itself
in the forms under which his actions are described. To
say that in the Gospels we have a series of anecdotes,
leading up to pointed sayings, is utterly beside the mark.
While the narrative forms of the time are adopted, they
are remodelled, often with a conscious reminiscence of
the language employed in scripture. In the Aramaic
originals these peculiarities of form would doubtless be
more pronounced. Semitic devices for giving elevation to ordinary narrative could not be reproduced in
Greek; turns of phrase which had solemn associations
could only be rendered by common words, or hinted at
by awkward additions. Thus in the forms of the Gospel record, as in its substance, we have to allow for a
new element, due to the Christian beliefs. A partial illustration may be drawn from the letters of Paul, which
are composed in the usual epistolary manner, with greet-
ings, compliments, thanksgivings—according to the con-
ventions of letter-writing in that age. Yet a new character is imposed on those forms by their association with
Christian ideas. We have likewise to allow for a re-
moulding of inherited forms when they were applied

to the purposes of the Christian tradition. Parallels derived from Rabbinical and other literatures are imperfect at the best, and for the most part misleading.

It is in connection with the Gospel history that the question of form has chiefly been discussed in recent years; but it has a bearing, perhaps still more important, on the record of Jesus' teaching. As we have them now the sayings have almost all a rhythmical, poetical character. They answer, in most instances, to the laws of Hebrew parallelism; and in addition to the brief sayings we occasionally have passages of some length which may be regarded as short poems (*e.g.* Mt. 6:25–33; 11:20–24; 11:25–30; 23:34–39). Their beauty is due not merely to the thought conveyed but to a structure of clauses and cadences which bears all the marks of conscious elaboration. Was it the custom of Jesus to express himself with this studied art? We can well believe that in his mode of speech there was something highly distinctive—a matchless clearness and concentration, a vividness of metaphor, a loftiness of thought which reflected itself in his language. The style in which his teaching is reported would not have been attributed to him unless it was in some degree characteristic. It has lately been proved that Boswell is himself responsible for much of the wording of Johnson's conversation; but he could not have made his hero speak in that manner unless it was reminiscent. The whole art consisted in making the man speak exactly as he might have spoken. This must have been equally true of sayings ascribed to Jesus by the early church. There were many people still living who had listened to Jesus, and well remembered his mode of teaching. They would perceive at once, by the very turn of phrase, whether any given utterance was really in character. No saying would find its way into the record unless it bore the intrinsic marks of the language of Jesus. Nevertheless it is difficult to believe that we have his sayings precisely in the words he used. What is evidently the same maxim has sometimes come to us in several versions, all of them different, although they all have the same characteristic note. The inference can hardly be avoided that the thought was preserved but was restated, by one teacher and another, in such terms as might have been used by Jesus. Not only so, but we have to reckon with a deliberate recasting in poetical form. This is not mere conjecture, for it is possible in some measure, by a comparison of the several Gospels, to trace the process by which given sayings were wrought into shape. The Beatitudes, for example, have a place both in Luke and Matthew, but the version in Matthew is clearly an advance on that in Luke. The four simple blessings are extended to seven or eight, and in all of them the language has become richer and more expressive. So the criticism of the old commandments is presented by Matthew in well-marked sections, which have some resemblance to regular strophes: the woes on the Pharisees are fully drawn out and worked to a climax, so that the whole chapter becomes a counterpart to the lyrical denunciations in

Amos and Isaiah. Jesus' teaching has been preserved, but has been invested, in a subsequent time, with a more imposing form.

It is not improbable that the single sayings have likewise undergone some change in their mode of expression. Many of them have the appearance of compressing into the fewest possible words what had been said at much greater length. We know from Mark that "without a parable he spoke nothing to them" (Mk. 4:34), and here we have no doubt a genuine reminiscence. Jesus habitually taught in parables, and a number of his parables have been recorded in full—each of them closing with a gnomic saying which gathers up its meaning. In some cases this has obviously been added by the reporter himself, since it betrays a misunderstanding of the parable; and as a rule the story conveys its own moral so lucidly that all explanation is superfluous. Yet we can easily see how the custom would arise of condensing an extended parable into its one main idea, which in some instances Jesus himself may have indicated in a few pregnant words at the close. Many of the sayings which survive may thus represent the final deposit of a great mass of parabolic teaching. It is hardly conceivable that Jesus regularly spoke in pointed maxims, one succeeding another without a break. Not only would such a mode of teaching have been unnatural but it would have been ineffectual. Nothing is more irritating than a string of epigrams, each one driving out the memory of the one before, and all of them suggesting a pose and a self-consciousness which would be utterly foreign to all that we know of Jesus. Those pregnant sayings which have come to us cannot have stood alone, but must represent the hammer-blows by which he finally drove home the truths he had been expounding.

Many of the sayings, therefore, may have been spoken by Jesus very much as we now have them. He may have added them to clinch the meaning of lost parables, or have thrown them out from time to time in the course of debate or conversation. It may be taken as certain, in view of the unanimous tradition, that he possessed in a very rare degree the gift of pungent expression. Things that he said would stick in the memory, and in the Gospels we have a selection of his most impressive sayings, remembered after his death. But it is difficult to account in this manner for all the sayings. Not only are they too numerous to have been carried in the memory word for word, but they seem to indicate by their form the work of later reflection. This does not mean that they are too perfectly expressed to have come out on the spur of the moment, for Jesus may well have uttered even more beautiful sayings than any that have come down to us. He instinctively put his thought into fitting words; and it must also be borne in mind that although he spoke without premeditation he had been pondering his message for years before he entered on his ministry. Nothing that he ever said was merely improvised. The problem before us does not concern the beauty of his language but the nature of its beauty. Those sayings are not framed in terms of ordinary speech. They are adapted to the acknowledged forms of Hebrew poetry, corresponding, in our own usage, to rhyme and rhythm; and it cannot be supposed that Jesus habitually spoke in that fashion. One of the chief marks of his teaching was its perfect naturalness. Listening to him the common people were able to feel that he spoke their own language, and thus made religion intelligible and real. They could not have so responded to him if he had always expressed his thoughts in studied, oracular terms.

It may therefore be assumed that in the process of transmission the sayings were remodelled. While the substance of the thought was retained, it was thrown into forms which defined it more sharply and at the same time made it easier to remember. This practice had already established itself in the Rabbinical schools, to which Christian teachers in early days must have looked for example. Each famous Rabbi was remembered by a few characteristic utterances, which summed up his teaching, or at least indicated its nature. Many of these maxims are preserved, and they betray a uniformity of pattern which cannot be entirely due to the teachers themselves. A technique had been developed in the Rabbinical schools for the transmission of important sayings; and the church apparently followed this practice. Jesus, it is true, had not taught like the scribes. There had been a freedom and originality in his thought which had also stamped itself on his mode of utterance, and the church sought, as far as possible, to reproduce his manner. Nevertheless, it employed a number of set forms in which the substance of his teaching could be preserved and handed down.

Our Gospels themselves provide evidence of the care which was bestowed on the formulation of the sayings. The evangelists make it their aim to record everything as they found it in their sources, but while doing so, they alter and improve. There is hardly a verse in which Matthew and Luke are in precise agreement. Sometimes a change is made on purely linguistic grounds, to correct the sentence in its grammar or phrasing. Sometimes the aim is greater clarity, or force, or conciseness. Sometimes the sense is modified, in order to replace an obscure thought by one which will be directly understood. It is doubtless true of all the evangelists that while adhering to their sources they exercise a conscious literary art; and Luke expressly tells us that this has been one of his objects. He prides himself on his "order"—meaning by this his careful arrangement, not only of the narrative as a whole, but of all the separate details. He has tried to put everything more succinctly, and so to do fuller justice to the tradition. Such, we may be sure, had always been the effort of the church teachers. In perfecting the form they did not conceive that they were doing any violence to the record. On the contrary they thought it part of their obligation to put into fitting shape what they had received. We expect of a good translator that he should give us not merely a faithful but an elegant version, and this was also regarded as the task of a good transmitter. He was required to convey the record intelligently, making the sense clear and effective, even when this involved a remodelling of the literal words. It rarely happens, even in these days of short-hand reporting, that a speech is printed exactly as it was delivered, with all the hesitations and repetitions and loosely strung sentences. If it is to impress the readers as it did the audience it must be put into some kind of readable shape. That, indeed, is the object of all literature and art—to impose those qualities of form which do not destroy but enhance the reality.

It may be granted, then, that we do not possess the *ipsissima verba* of Jesus. Occasionally he may have uttered a sentence so brief and arresting that it rang for years afterwards in the memory of his hearers exactly as he had spoken it. But in far the greater number of sayings this cannot be assumed. No one, so far as we know, took notes of Jesus' teaching. It was entrusted to the memory, and words remembered very quickly lose their original form. Great importance has usually been attached to the time that may have elapsed between the utterance and the writing down of Jesus' sayings; but this element of time is, after all, a secondary one. Even a week or a single day after Jesus had spoken, men would be doubtful as to what he had said, and would report him differently. May we not discover an actual proof of this in one outstanding instance? At the trial before the Council it was all-important to make sure of the very words in which Jesus had declared that in three days he could rebuild the temple. This was the crucial "blasphemy" on which the accusation hinged,

and several witnesses were brought in, who had heard
the words spoken, only a day or two before. The Council was eager to have their evidence, and they had probably been hired for the express purpose of obtaining it;
yet they could not be made to agree on what Jesus had
actually said (Mk. 64:58, 59). Must it not have been
the same with nearly all the sayings? The Gospels are
constantly at variance in their record, and this was inevitable. What Jesus literally said on any given occasion can never be ascertained—not because the account
was not written down until years afterwards, but because
it had never been uniform. The witnesses, like those at
the trial, had differed from each other from the very
start. It is sometimes argued, on this ground, that we
cannot know anything of the actual teaching of Jesus.[4]
Those sayings which we attribute to him were not
strictly his own. As they came down through the community they were expressed in new language, and were
revised and edited, so that the real message is irretriev-
ably lost. We call our religion by the name of Jesus,
but there can be no certainty that at any point we have
direct contact with him. At first sight the argument
might seem to destroy all confidence in the Gospel record, but it would apply with equal force to any record
that has ever been. Words have been attributed to every
famous man which have made him a living figure to
succeeding times, but which do not correspond to what
he literally said. One thinks, for instance, of Luther's
great defiance at the Diet of Worms. Undoubtedly he

[4]*Cf.* C. A. H. Guignebert, *Christianity*, ch. I.

made that defiance, but his words have come to us in four or five accounts which differ from each other, and no one can tell whether any of them is correct. It is seldom, indeed, that any man can repeat quite accurately what he himself said on some given occasion. He knows what he intended; he remembers the general tenor of his words; but when you try to fasten him down to any precise statement he can only say, "It must have been something like that." This is also the furthest we can go with regard to any of the recorded words of Jesus. We know that the church accepted these words as having been spoken by him. We need not doubt that the thought was his, even though he may not have expressed it in just those terms. If it is argued that the different versions of a saying are proof that he never uttered it, we may fairly answer that they prove the very opposite. Several reporters are agreed that he spoke to that effect; and if they differ as to the words we can be all the more certain of the thought conveyed.

Thus the church inherited a large number of sayings which purported to be those of Jesus. They had been transmitted in different versions, but this was not due to any tampering with the record, or to the fading out of authentic memories through lapse of time. The differences had always existed, and could not but arise when spoken words were reported by various witnesses. It was not so much the words as the teaching of Jesus which the church was anxious to preserve, and for this reason it allowed itself a certain freedom. Sayings ascribed to him were sometimes recast, to make them more pointed and explicit. What he had spoken at considerable length was often compressed into a single maxim. Out of a whole discourse or parable only the one sentence that contained the significant idea was preserved. These changes were all made with the purpose of elucidating the message of Jesus, by clearing it of all that seemed irrelevant, and stating it in plainer and more forcible language; and the church took a yet further liberty with its tradition. It threw the original records into certain patterns, sometimes with the aid of rhythmical devices. This would appear to have been the chief modification which the church made on what it had received from the immediate witnesses, and the purpose of these "forms" has now to be considered.[5]

[5]The literature of "Formgeschichte" is now extensive and is constantly growing. Among the works of special value are: M. Dibelius (translated by B. Lee Woolf), *From Tradition to Gospel*; E. Fascher, *Die Formgeschichtliche Methode* (critical as well as expository); M. Albertz, *Die Synoptische Streitgespräche*; R. Bultmann, *Geschichte der Synoptischen Tradition* and *Die Erforschung der syn. Evangelien*; B. S. Easton, *The Gospel before the Gospels*; V. Taylor, *The Formation of Gospel Tradition*; F. C. Grant, *Form Criticism* (a translation of two outstanding German contributions).

CHAPTER VI

THE MEANING OF FORM

THE investigation of form has marked a real advance in Gospel criticism. It may be that too much has been claimed for the new method, and that most of its findings are premature, and will always remain, in a greater or less degree, conjectural. But at least a crevice has been opened through which we can see some little way into that background of oral tradition which lies behind our documents. If nothing has been positively discovered a number of probabilities have come to light which may lead, in course of time, to solid results.[1]

The temptation hitherto has been to confuse the facts obtained by the new method with theories which are more than doubtful. Too often, indeed, theory is used as an instrument for determining the facts. It is assumed that the tradition arose out of the cult or doctrine or practice of the Christian community, and the forms are adjusted to this supposition. In the framing of a myth to suit its requirements the church must have been guided by certain principles, and we can thus discover the laws by which the record was formulated. Wherever it conflicts with these laws it must be set aside, or undergo the necessary correction.

[1]The value of the method has been admirably explained by B. S. Easton in his two books, *The Gospel before the Gospels*, and *Christ in the Gospels*. He also indicates some of its limitations.

Even when the facts are obtained by legitimate critical methods, conclusions are sometimes drawn from
them which are purely fanciful, and are yet passed off,
by a sleight of hand, as part of the criticism. The literary structure of the records is made a ground for assess-
ing their historical and religious value. It is claimed that
by mere analysis of their form we can tell that most of
the narratives of Jesus are imaginary, or in any case
were mainly fashioned by the community itself out of
a few very slight recollections. The form in which any
episode has come to us is now accepted by some scholars
as the criterion by which a judgment may be passed on
its historical substance.[2] This, however, is highly ques-
tionable. It may be granted that the literary character
of a document is, to some extent, a clue to its value.
From a composition which on the face of it is poetical
we do not look for the same accuracy as in a work of
prose. If the language used is that of a given period we
accept the document as good evidence for the history of
that period. A diary or private letter is more to be relied on than a pamphlet, written obviously in some party
interest. Yet the worth of the contents cannot be judged
from the form alone. A song or ballad may be better
history than a set chronicle. A late work may be nearer
to the facts than one written by a contemporary. Official
statements need to be checked as well as popular tales
and casual anecdotes. The forms of the Gospel narrative must indeed be taken into account; but on this evi-

[2] M. Dibelius (*Die Botschaft von Jesus Christus*) has sought to reconstruct
the original message by applying the supposed laws of form to the record as
we now have it.

dence alone it is impossible to base any historical judgment.

One fact in particular has emerged from the modern criticism, and might seem, at first sight, to rule out all claims of the record to be considered as history. The forms in which it is cast are demonstrably artificial. It cannot, therefore, have reached us in its original state but has passed through a process in which various factors have played their part. Must we not conclude that this is true of the substance as it is of the form? These accounts of the work of Jesus have been mediated by the life and reflection of the early community. It used the memory of Jesus as a sort of screen on which it projected its own experiences, and in this manner devised a series of episodes which have the appearance of being authentic, but the illusion can be detected when we observe the artificial character of the forms. A story which wears the manifest garb of fiction may reasonably be presumed to be more fiction than fact.

Different theories have been put forward to account for the narrative which thus purports to be the life of Jesus; and some of them have already been examined. We have seen that the whole idea of the community as itself creating the record is due, in the main, to loose thinking and a loose employment of language. The term "community" is equivalent to the symbol "x," and merely denotes that everything must be explained by causes of which we know nothing. There is no evidence that the community in any way invented or distorted the record. Everything would appear to show that its action was conservative. A record transmitted through individuals might fairly be suspected, but one that was used constantly in the public worship of a community was safe-guarded. There could be no more effective check on any attempt to deviate from a received tradition.

No one, indeed, would maintain that the record has come to us through a purely colourless medium. Jesus, for the early church, was the Messiah, who had won salvation for his people and to whom they looked for present guidance. His life could not be treated merely as an interesting chapter of bygone history. The object of the church in recalling it was to strengthen faith in Jesus, and to make his example effectual; and this practical purpose is never forgotten in our Gospels. Their narrative is to this extent determined by the conditions which prevailed in the Christian community. But it must never be forgotten that those conditions which are reflected in the history had themselves been created by the work of Jesus. We do not argue that the career of Julius Cæsar must be fictitious because the Roman Empire had somehow come into being and needed to postulate a man of that kind as its founder. If the Empire was based on ideas which it ascribed to Cæsar, the natural assumption is that Cæsar was a real person, who originated those ideas and with them the Empire which preserved his story. And when we find a community which called itself by the name of Jesus and sought to order its life by his precepts, we may conclude that its account of him is substantially true. There is no fair ground for a theory that the church in some mysterious way grew up of its own accord, and then compiled a legend, explaining how it came to be.

Assuming, then, that the record is historical, how are we to interpret those forms in which it was embodied, and which are still traceable under the Greek of our Gospels? In the narrative portions they consist of little more than an order, relatively fixed, in which the elements of each story are placed. In the teaching we have to do with something that approaches a poetical form. Some of the sayings are highly elaborated, and even in the Greek suggest a rhythm, which was probably much more pronounced in the Aramaic. This feature of the record plainly goes back to the period before the tradition was put into writing. Our evangelists had found it in their sources, and it was characteristic of all the sources, and must have been present in the original material out of which they were made. They were transcriptions, as may be gathered from Luke's prelude, of the primitive testimony—that is, of the oral tradition. Formerly it could only be said that the tradition was at first handed down by word of mouth, and to this statement it could be added that this tradition, as orally delivered, was not continuous, but was made up of a number of short, detached pieces. Now we are in a position to say that the pieces were constructed in a particular manner, each of them with a stated outline and content.

Before considering the significance of these forms it is necessary to meet the contention that a narrative which is couched in artificial forms cannot be in harmony with facts. Reflection and manipulation have plainly been at work in the framing of the various episodes. Does not this throw suspicion on their whole character? Those who fashioned the vehicle would take similar liberties with the things conveyed. But this does not follow. Nothing more can be inferred from the nature of the forms than that the church was accustomed to tell stories of Jesus in a particular way. The stories themselves might be true or false, but it was expected that they should be thrown into this approved mould. We have here no singularity of the early church, which calls for ingenious theories to account for it. If the methods of any narrator were examined it would be found that all his stories, however they may differ in character, have a family likeness. He has developed his own technique in story-telling, and applies it to all kinds of material— to what he has himself witnessed as well as to things he has imagined. For that part, the form is usually most rigid when the narrative is most matter-of-fact. One has only to think of a business letter, a captain's log-book, a policeman's evidence in court, a scientific demonstration. Nothing could be more conventional than these statements. They are framed, in every instance, on exactly the same pattern, for the simple reason that they set forth the facts required in what has proved to be the necessary order. It would not be too much to say that artificial form, so far from throwing doubt on the things stated, is the mark of veracity. This has been understood by all writers who have tried to give an air of realism to a narrative that is pure invention. Defoe, for example, is the most convincing of story-tellers because he has mastered the art of constructing his tales as formal documents. The reader cannot but believe that a narrative which is so faithful in every particular to some conventional manner must be true.

Perhaps it was for this reason that in ancient story-telling the form was much more regular than it is now. There were certain schemes to which every record had to adapt itself, and the reader expected to have the facts presented to him in just that way. He was put out when the familiar formulæ were omitted, and the events were not unfolded in the customary order. In the East, more especially, the methods of narrative were strictly prescribed. The frame was not fitted to the picture but the picture to the frame. If this is true of the Gospel narratives it is equally true of the Old Testament stories, of the Arabian tales, of the chronicles of Egyptian and Persian kings. To our minds the forms appear artificial, but to those for whom they were intended they were natural, and a loose, flexible mode of narration would have caused misgivings. A story did not appear credible unless it was told in the fixed order, according to the set rules.

The forms of the Gospel tradition afford no proof that it is not historical, and we may go further. The form is a guarantee of the contents and was imposed for that very purpose. For a generation the record was transmitted orally, and was at the mercy of every accident. Every one who told the story of Jesus was at liberty to add and omit and modify, and there was no standard by which the alterations could be checked. It is only too apparent that an oral record, after many such repetitions by different people, would become so changed that even the main drift of it could hardly be recovered. This is evident to us now, and negative criticism has made the most of it; but it would be still more evident to members of the primitive church. Again and again they would hear the story which they had heard in one version told shortly afterwards in quite another; and the need of preserving some consistency would force itself on them for urgent reasons both of faith and practice. How was this consistency to be secured? The one certain method was to commit the record to writing, and eventually this method was adopted; but so long as it was deemed necessary to adhere to oral tradition only one device was possible. The message which had been delivered in loose, improvised language must be invested with a stated form. This would serve a double purpose. On the one hand it made the facts easy to remember. Instead of a diffuse account there would be a brief compact one, in which the essential points were selected, and placed in a uniform order, so that each of them would suggest the one that followed. On the other hand—and this was much more important—the fixed form would act as a safe-guard. If it was not observed the listeners would at once recognise that something had been added or left out. The form bound down the narrator to the one accepted version of the facts.

That this was one main object of the forms which

are traceable in the Gospel tradition is more than probable, and is borne out by many analogies. We find that invariably, when the aid of writing is not available, some kind of form has been used as a substitute. Much of the poetry of early times had its origin in a utilitarian motive. The metrical form was employed to give permanence to things that needed to be remembered, and at the same time to preserve them from alteration. Laws were drawn up in a rude rhythm; thinkers expressed their cardinal ideas in verse, which their disciples would commit to memory; kings and cities had their official poets, whose duty it was to chronicle famous events and pass them on securely to following generations. In all these instances the same two motives can be discerned— to assist the memory, and to stabilise the approved version of things that mattered. Order and language were now fixed, and into such a record it was difficult to introduce any changes. With a similar motive the church put its tradition into form. For passages of narrative it was enough to arrange the facts according to a given scheme, which ensured that they should come in the right order and lead up to the truth or warning they were meant to enforce. The narrator was held within bounds, and his hearers were made aware when he brought in anything that had no proper place in the story. For the preservation of the teaching more definite forms were necessary. The sayings of Jesus were reproduced in poetical modes of speech, resembling those of the prophets and the authors of the Wisdom literature. He himself had probably spoken in this manner only on rare occasions, and it is more than likely that his words as we have them bear the impress of the later church. None the less, the object was to preserve what he had really taught. He had used the common language, and if he had done otherwise the common people would not have heard him gladly; but for the purpose of transmission this language was unfitted. When you report a familar conversation you put the sense of it into different words, and with the change of words there is always some distortion. After several repetitions the sense is lost, as well as the original language. If the thought of Jesus was to be preserved it had to be transposed out of the language he had employed into sententious utterance which had a set form. The memory could now take a firm hold of the saying, and the idea contained in it was clearly defined, and could not easily be perverted. It is a curious logic which finds evidence in the forms that the church wilfully corrupted its record, and ascribed to Jesus its own reflections and beliefs. The natural conclusion is just the opposite. By means of form the church deliberately put a curb on its own fancy. It was conscious that the teaching of Jesus, so long as it was freely repeated, was liable to a constant process of modification. Pains were therefore taken to preserve the various sayings by fixing them. The forms are our security that the teaching of Jesus has been transmitted, not perhaps in his literal words, but in the sense which it conveyed to the earliest believers.

At this point, however, several questions of the highest importance fall to be considered. (1) In the first place, when did the imposition of form begin? To this question no definite answer is possible; but it may be said generally that forms would be adopted when the danger of corruption had become apparent, but could still be overcome. At the outset the account of Jesus would be delivered by eyewitnesses in any language that came to them at the moment. It could be taken for granted that these men who had been in Jesus' company would report him correctly, and no one would demand that they would always repeat themselves in the same words. But a time came when the accounts began to deviate. Different teachers would give conflicting versions of what they had heard from Peter and John; and perhaps these Apostles would sometimes contradict themselves. It was felt necessary to decide, once for all, in what manner some particular story should be told, and one version was agreed on, and was fixed in appropriate form. The process would be carried out very gradually. We are not to imagine that the church, on a certain day, decided that its whole record should be put into form, and appointed a committee for this purpose. Things were not done in that fashion in the primitive church. The process of formulation would extend over years, and would be applied to one portion of the record and another, as the need arose. But the transposition into form, however it was effected, may be taken to mark the true beginning of a Gospel literature. It is customary to make a division between the period of oral tradition and that of written documents. The record which had previously been fluid was put into writing, and this is supposed to be the grand turning-point in the history of the tradition. From this time on we are clear of the quaking bog and can feel solid ground beneath our feet. But the real division ought to be made farther back, at the time when the floating tradition was thrown into forms. The distinction between word of mouth and writing is, after all, an arbitrary one, since the writers merely set down what was already crystallised. We date the Homeric poems and the Icelandic sagas from the time when they were composed by poetic craftsmen. It was then that they became literature—not at the time, perhaps centuries later, when they were committed to paper. The origin of the Gospel literature ought to be dated in the same way.

(2) Another question which cannot but suggest itself is that of the agency by which the tradition was reduced to form. The work is credited to the community, and in view of our blank ignorance it is impossible to speak with greater precision. But we must be careful to guard against the idea, which in recent years has been such a fruitful source of error, that the record in some way shaped itself automatically. The more we study any fragment of it, the more we realise that we have before us a piece of art, which could not have come into being by some happy accident. There must have been teachers in the church who not only repeated but deliberately shaped the tradition. Who they were we shall never know; but it is evident that they must have given time and reflection to the work, which is performed, for the

most part, with exquisite skill. Any one who studies our Gospels in a Synopsis is aware how every phrase and word in the sources has been carefully weighed; and the authors of the sources would follow a similar method, and likewise the teachers before them who put the record into form. It is necessary to remind ourselves again that the early disciples were not barbarians, as we are far too apt to assume, but belonged to a cultured age, and to a nation in which literary expression had been carried to high perfection. Among its teachers the church would have men who well understood the finer uses of language, and to such men we owe the casting of those forms which not only ensured the permanence of the records but have won them a place among the world's great literature.

It can hardly be doubted that the chief object of formulation was to preserve and fix the tradition, but this implies a further motive. Whenever form is applied to matters which have hitherto been conveyed in ordinary speech, we may infer that the thing so treated is valuable. From the mass of common facts or ideas a selection has been made, and what is deemed most important has been set aside, and expressed in such language that it will be remembered. This, for example, was the origin of all popular proverbs. They were devised, in an early stage of society, as finger-posts for the conduct of life. From time to time a principle was observed which was eminently true and helpful, and it was put into arresting words, so that it might stand out from the confusion of opinions. This also was the motive at work in the making of popular songs. Events were singled out which were worth remembering; thoughts and emotions were recognised which were richer in quality than those of every-day existence. Poetry, by Matthew Arnold's definition, is a criticism of life. Perhaps it might be defined more accurately as a selection from life—an effort to sift out from common experience the things of lasting value. Form always implies a selection. Just as we set apart our more precious belongings and keep them in drawers or boxes, so we instinctively enclose in forms the ideas and memories and sentiments which we are most anxious to preserve. And this, it may be presumed, was one main reason why form was employed in the treatment of the Gospel tradition. Out of all that was known or rumored of the life and teaching of Jesus the church laid hold of those things which it most desired to keep. These, at least, must be made secure. They were fundamental to any true conception of what Jesus had been, and of what he had taught and done.

It is generally assumed that the church has transmitted to us in the Gospels almost all that it ever knew about Jesus. The modern investigation is to a great extent built on this assumption, which passes, as a rule, without challenge. We are asked to believe that after his death the memory of Jesus quickly faded. Occupied as it was with what it conceived to be his message the church lost sight of Jesus himself; he had become a shadowy figure even in the first generation, and after it was passed very little was remembered of his actual life.

Then it was suddenly realised that unless some effort was made the facts about him would be forgotten altogether, and the church set itself diligently to collect the fragments of reminiscence which still survived. These were now few and meagre, but everything that could be discovered was scraped together, and these scanty gleanings were eked out with doubtful hearsay. Thus our Gospels came into existence—made up of miscellaneous materials, for the most part of inferior value, but containing all that could possibly be ascertained of Jesus in the succeeding age. So in each new Life of Jesus it is impressed on us that the attempt to make anything like a biography is well-nigh hopeless, since we have nothing to go by but those scraps of information which, by some accident, escaped the wreck.

It is worth suggesting that this theory, for which there is no evidence whatever, ought to be reversed. Our Gospels, so far from containing everything that could be discovered by the most diligent scrutiny, are the final outcome of a long process of selection. This is more than a hypothesis, for the Gospels consist for the most part of episodes and sayings which had been invested with form, at a time previous to any written documents. Form implies selection, and the inference may be fairly drawn that a large mass of material was available. Many who had known Jesus were still living, and all Christians were eager to hear from them whatever they could tell. There will be occasion to return later to this neglected aspect of the tradition, but at present it is enough to note that memories of Jesus were in the first age plentiful. We have in our Gospels not the record which the church was compelled to give, for want of anything better, but that which it chose to give. From all that it possessed it selected those things which appeared to be best worth preserving.

What were the motives which determined the selection? It might have been expected that the most significant acts and sayings would at once be evident, and would naturally take their place in the regular tradition. To a considerable extent this is what happened, and some things are included in all the Gospels, just as there are twenty or thirty hymns which cannot be omitted from any collection. Yet it is surprising that many episodes to which we now attach the highest value are passed over by one or other of the evangelists, though it is almost certain that he must have known them. On the other hand, things that seem to us relatively unimportant, for instance some of the miracle stories, are found in all the Gospels. This, perhaps, is the chief argument for the theory that little was known. If there was a copious tradition, why is the selection not made with more discernment? Every anthology, however, is liable to the same criticism. We look in vain for the extracts we should certainly have chosen, and find them replaced by others, which to our mind could have been left out. This only means that one man's choice will always differ from another's; and it must also be remembered that our attitude today is not that of the primitive church. The Gospels were drawn up for their own age, with its peculiar standards of what was valuable. They were intended, too, for practical use in a miscellaneous community. If the evangelists had been entirely free they might have done their work differently; but they had to consider the needs of the church and the variety of people included in it. Their selection is, in some sense, an official one, and must be judged from that point of view.

It must be noted, too, that when our Gospels were composed the selection was, in large measure, already made. Parts of the record had been separated from the rest and put into form, and were in general use at the church meetings. What the evangelists have done is, in the main, to combine in a coherent whole the passages which had commended themselves to the judgment of the church. We have to put ourselves in the position of the early teachers, and enquire what motives would weigh with them when they selected certain parts of the material which lay to their hands, and threw them into form—by this means securing that they should be preserved and handed down.

(1) The existing conditions of the church would doubtless count for much. From the words and examples of Jesus the brethren sought direction for the conduct of daily life, for the solution of urgent problems, for the administration of worship and of the communal life. Preference would be given to acts and sayings of Jesus which appeared to bear more immediately on those present needs, and in the formulation of such passages a turn would often be given them which made their application more obvious. This was natural, and it can be

demonstrated in not a few instances that this has been done. But the passages themselves, though they may have been modified, belonged to the record, and were selected in view of their fitness to a special purpose.

(2) Preference would be given to incidents which lent confirmation to the beliefs of the church, and especially the central belief that Jesus was the Messiah. This has manifestly been one of the guiding principles of the selection. As the scriptures were searched for predictions of Jesus' Messiahship, so was the record for incidents that seemed to reveal him in his Messianic character. From the prominence of this motive it has been held that the Gospels are little more than theological pamphlets in the guise of history; and the view is justified to this extent—that a doctrinal motive has largely determined the selection. Many things were known about Jesus which in themselves were more valuable than some which have been preserved; but they had no apparent bearing on that belief which controlled the life of the church, and they were allowed to go. The scope of the Gospels has in some ways been narrowed by this concentration on the Messianic belief. This is apparent when Luke is compared with the more arid narratives of Mark and Matthew. Luke, writing for the Gentile church, has in large measure broken away from the Messianism of Palestinian Christianity. He has learned to think of Jesus as the messenger of peace and human brotherhood, and is able to bring in a whole mass of material which we now regard as the most precious in the Gospels. This is commonly set down to his pos-

session of sources which were unknown to the other two evangelists, but perhaps it would be nearer the truth to say that he has been less limited in his selection. Setting before himself a wider purpose he has been able to admit from the current tradition a great deal that the others have purposely omitted.

(3) It would be wrong, however, to think of the early teachers as concerned wholly with the passing needs of the community and the doctrines on which it took its stand. They were fully awake to the spiritual value of the story of Jesus, and to the newness and splendour of his teaching. Our Gospels are full of passages which only by a forced ingenuity can be construed as topical. If they were significant for the early church they are no less so for earnest men and women in all ages. It is the evident aim of those who drew up the record to preserve whatever they can of what was most distinctive in the work of Jesus. Emphasis is continually laid on the contrast between his teaching and the practices and beliefs which had hitherto prevailed. He is set before us as the prototype of a new humanity, the pioneer of a new and better way of obedience to God. It is utterly unjust to the early Christians to conceive of them as wholly occupied with doctrinal shibboleths and the regulations of their own little group. For the members of the primitive church, as for the church in all ages, Christianity meant a new approach to God, a new outlook on life. We cannot but realise, as we read the First Epistle of Peter, the thirteenth chapter of I Corinthians, the Supper Discourses in the Fourth Gospel, that the imitation

of Christ was the primary interest in the Christian religion. It had been so from the very first, and we cannot understand why the Gospels were written unless we take account of this motive, more than of any other. The record was intended to inspire and direct Christ's followers by the example of Christ. A selection was made of actions which made him real as a personality, and words which illustrated most clearly his mode of thought.

(4) Nearly half the space in each Gospel is occupied with the account of Jesus' death, with all its accompanying circumstances. There are various indications that the Passion story was originally a unit by itself; and this was inevitable, since the death of Christ was the chief theme of missionary teaching. Paul had resolved not to know Christ after the flesh, but he himself tells that he was wont to describe, as in a vivid picture, how Christ had died (Gal. 3:1). To Paul we owe our primary evidence on the two great episodes of the Lord's Supper and the Resurrection. Intent as he was on the inner meanings of the Christian message he placed a cardinal value on the facts, and we cannot but be struck with the preciseness of detail in his historical statements. They read almost like official declarations, and Paul indicates that this was indeed their nature by the terms in which he quotes them. "I delivered what also I received" (I Cor. 15:3). "Whether it be I or they, thus we teach" (I Cor. 15:11). It may almost be said that in these passages of Paul we find the earliest examples of how form was applied to the Gospel record. Primary episodes of

the history are presented in a brief recitative, in which the main facts are carefully chosen out and succinctly put together.

The Passion story, then, appears to have been the first part of the narrative which was treated in this manner, and here we can trace the operation of all the motives we have been considering. For the purpose of church worship, which centred in the commemoration of the Lord's death, it was necessary to have a plain record of how the death had taken place. Since the death of Jesus was his crowning Messianic work, all the facts concerning it had to be clearly set forth. And since the church looked to Jesus as its teacher and example it was bound to remember his death, in which everything he had taught was gathered up in one supreme act. Thus in the selection from the record the first place was given to that portion of it on which all the rest depended. The account of the life became only a prelude to that of the death, and is meant to be considered in the light of it. Many readers have observed that nothing in the Gospels is recounted with such austerity and simplicity as this story of the Passion. This is especially striking in Mark's narrative, and the inference has sometimes been drawn that the purpose of his Gospel is not historical but ritual or theological. Everything is told in bare outline—with no attempt to rouse emotion—no appreciation, one might think, of the great human tragedy. But this character of the narrative can be explained when we think of it as composed with a definite object. The account of the Passion was the fundamental part of the record, and was also that part of it which lent itself most easily to fanciful accretions. This is apparent from the later mythology of the church, and from the extravagant details which have crept into the versions even of Luke and Matthew. It was imperative that the facts should be recalled, just as they had happened. The death of Christ was the central theme of the Christian message, and all teachers were left free to make their own theories as to its significance. But the facts must not be confused with any myth or speculation. Since everything else rested on them they must be set forth exactly as they were. So in his accounts of the Supper and the Resurrection Paul confines himself to a mere summary, one might almost say a catalogue, of certain things which had been vouched for by the immediate witnesses. He discerns a profound religious meaning in those events, and is preparing the way for its exposition. But before he can proceed any further he feels it necessary to state, as exactly as he can, the historical facts. This is also the motive in that plain chronicle, so impressive because of its utter simplicity, in which Mark recounts the story of the Passion.

These are some of the reasons which must have weighed with the church when it selected a number of episodes from the life of Jesus, and gave them permanence by means of form. But was there not a further reason? May we not believe that Christian teachers were anxious to transmit a record which, to the best of their knowledge, was authentic? It is strange that this possibility should hardly be entertained by many recent writers. They work on the assumption that the church took no trouble whatever with its tradition. Some things were remembered about Jesus, but purely by accident. Legendary material was admitted as freely as fact—indeed more freely, since it allowed more scope for those doctrinal and communal interests which were all that really mattered. It is taken for granted that until our own time no effort was ever made to sift out the true elements of the history. Now on the face of it this conception of the attitude of the early church is incredible. Since Jesus was the object of faith there must have been some desire to know what he had actually done while he lived on earth. In all times since there has been an intense curiosity about his life; even the wild fables which began to spring up as early as the second century are proof of this interest in him. It must have been at least as strong in the age following his death, when first-hand information was still available. As we have seen already, the absorption in his message cannot have displaced the interest in his life, for the two things were inseparable. The message consisted in nothing else than the proclamation that the Messiah had at last appeared, and every one must have wanted to know how he had appeared, and what he had done that proved him to be Messiah. It must also be borne in mind (and this is a point too often forgotten) that even if the church was disposed to forget the facts the unbelieving world forbade it to do so. The whole point of the Jewish attack was that Jesus, in his known career, did not fulfil the

Messianic conditions. One fact after another was brought forward and exploited to the utmost, which threw doubt on his claims. Malicious stories were invented, which could only be countered by a statement of the facts. One of the chief cares of the church was to neutralise these attacks, which were directed not so much against Christian doctrine as against the character and action of Jesus himself. Of this we have striking evidence in the Fourth Gospel, with its constant polemic against the slanders and misconceptions of "the Jews." It is evident that Jewish criticism, in the evangelist's time, had fastened on the historical career of Jesus, and he feels it necessary to deal with the various objections. This, perhaps, is one of the chief reasons why his work, theological in its nature, takes the form of history. He is aware that Christian ideas cannot be presented in a true light unless the facts of Jesus' life are cleared of all doubts and aspersions.[3] A similar task was imposed on Christian teachers from the first. The easiest method of attacking the Christian mission was to spread discreditable rumours about Jesus himself. These could not be answered by mere fables, in a time so near to the events; and those who believed in Jesus had no choice but to inform themselves of the facts and make them known.

Thus it was a matter of practical concern to the church to become acquainted with the history. It was not enough to form some hazy imaginative picture of Jesus,

---

[3]W. Wrede (*Charakter und Tendenz des Johannischen Evangeliums*) draws attention to the prominence, in early controversy, of attacks on the personal history of Jesus.

for there was always the danger that ignorant statements would be challenged. There was, moreover, on the part of Christians, a deep desire to know more of Jesus and to learn all the facts correctly. This we may infer from Luke's preface to his Gospel. His friend Theophilus had already passed through a course of instruction, in which he had received knowledge of Jesus, but he wished to know more, and to make sure that the information given him could be relied on. Luke offers him the results of a full historical enquiry. He takes Theophilus as typical of all intelligent converts, and presents them with a book from which "they may know with certainty the things in which they had been instructed" (Lk. 1:4).

This, then, it may be maintained, was one motive, and not the least cogent, in the selection that was made from the miscellaneous record. In the course of those years when all teaching was by word of mouth it was difficult to make sure that the facts were rightly transmitted. Much that passed as information was mere hearsay. Reminiscence had become coloured by imagination. Things in themselves authentic had been wrested from their proper meaning. The church was aware that the record was in danger of perversion, and was anxious to know what it could believe. It was in this interest, more, perhaps, than in any other, that form was applied to a number of episodes in the history. Here were some things which were well authenticated. Amidst all that was doubtful the church could hold firmly to these elements in its tradition, which might serve as a touch-stone for everything else. It is noteworthy that most of the narratives which bear the impress of form are, on the face of them, credible. Allowing for the tendency, natural to the ancient world, to explain remarkable events as miracles, there is very little in the Marcan narrative which might not have happened. We can feel at every point that this was how the disciples, after some lapse of time, would recall the events they had witnessed. This, it may be surmised, was the chief motive which guided Christian teachers in their work of selection. When the tradition had been duly sifted it was found that for some parts of it there was adequate authority. It might almost be claimed that the teachers who put the record into form were the earliest critics of the Gospel history. In their own fashion they had examined the material and placed their stamp of approval on that which they found trustworthy.

It is not to be supposed that the tests which they employed were of just the same kind as we should use now. As yet there was no clear conception of the laws of historical evidence, no means of determining whether an event was possible within the order of nature. Yet we may credit these early investigators with an honest desire to trace back each report to its source. If the Apostles themselves were no longer accessible there were those who had listened to them, and could vouch for what they had said. Papias may be mistaken when he tells us that Mark recorded what he had heard from Peter; but his statement at least preserves the memory of how conscientious teachers in the early days had gone about their work—seeking their knowledge from those who could give it at first hand. Papias himself tried to continue this practice when he sought out the "elders," and enquired of them what they had heard from the disciples of the Lord.[4] We may believe, too, that the early teachers would compare the current versions of incidents and sayings, and so arrive at their judgment as to which one should be preferred. This has been the method followed by our evangelists. They all adopt it as a matter of course, and from this we may gather that it was already in common use. When they are unable to make a choice between two alternatives they make room for both, and this custom also may date back to the early time.

It may be concluded, then, that form was employed to give permanence and stability to the tradition, and that it also points to a selection of those parts of the tradition which the church, for a variety of reasons, was most anxious to preserve. The forms, however, have a further significance. They plainly suggest that the passages so treated were meant for public recital. Literary modes of expression are always used in order to give proper dignity to some public utterance, and in ancient times the distinction between formal and colloquial language was much more marked than it is now. If the Gospel records are formally constructed they must have been meant for publicity, and this could only be secured in the early church by recital at the church meeting. It seems evident, when we examine the separate passages contained in our Gospels, that they were

[4]Eusebius III:39.

intended for this purpose. Each of them is an independent unit complete in itself. They are approximately of the same length. They lend themselves to impressive delivery, as every one feels today when they are read out in the church service. We know that the books of the Law were divided, for use in the synagogue, into brief sections, one for each Sabbath in a cycle of three years. It may be that a somewhat similar practice was adopted in the worship of the early church. A series of scripture passages would be read, according to a regular scheme—each of them followed by the recital of a given episode from the life of Jesus.

If the sections of the record were designed for the church meeting we have a strong guarantee that they were framed carefully, with a full sense of responsibility. They were to be repeated, time after time, before the assembled brotherhood. The recital of them was to rank as an act of worship, and nothing that was false or unworthy could be admitted. It must be remembered, too, that the community itself was the chief safeguard of the purity of the tradition. Some one would certainly be present at every meeting who would know the facts and would protest against any statement that was plainly wrong. Those who had the shaping of the Gospel record would be constantly mindful that their work would be severely tested, and would take pains to transmit faithfully what they knew, on good evidence, to be true.

CHAPTER VII

THE BEGINNING OF THE TRADITION

OUR Gospels represent the final outcome of a long process, which can be traced backward, up to a certain point, with a fair degree of confidence. It can be shown that Matthew and Luke made use of writings which themselves had some literary pretensions. One of them was our Gospel of Mark, in which a number of primitive records were brought together and carefully arranged in sequence, so as to make a coherent narrative. Mark was only one of the "many" early works to which Luke admits his indebtedness, and which were presumably of a similar character. They were composed in Greek, and aimed at the collection and arrangement of earlier material. Their authors had found the preliminary work done for them. They had only to put together a number of episodes and sayings which had been selected, and thrown into proper language, and perhaps roughly grouped according to subject.

Before any of these documents came into existence there was a period in which all records of Jesus must have consisted of detached pieces, preserved in an oral tradition. In the light of recent investigation we are able to penetrate some little way into that dim period. There is evidence that at some date when it was still in the oral phase the tradition was reduced to form. Stories about Jesus were cast in a given mould; his sayings were condensed into pointed maxims, or were invested with poetical rhythm. Here we can discover the first attempt to give fixity to the record. Although it was still transmitted orally it was adjusted to patterns which secured for it something of the permanence which we associate with literature. This formulation of the record, although it was effected gradually, must have begun within a very few years after Jesus' death. Paul quotes several sayings of Jesus which have all the characteristics of form, and which he assumes to be familiar to his readers. He likewise recounts two historical episodes in language which plainly suggests a formal statement, intended for public recitation. From the time that the record thus began to be formulated we can trace a continuous development. Later teachers took up the work of their predecessors and sought with extended means to preserve and fix the tradition.

But when the record has thus been traced backward as far as we can go, we are still left with a period in which everything was unstable. How long it may have lasted we cannot tell; but even if it may be contracted to a few years there was time enough for the tradition to become fatally obscured. The critic of the Gospels, however far he may push back his sources, has finally to reckon with that dark interval in which all was at the mercy of popular rumour. The memories even of eye-witnesses must often have played them false; authentic stories must have grown distorted, and fables may have crept in under guise of fact. This interval, however short, when there was no fixed record, must always remain the crux of Gospel enquiry. All experience proves that even a few months or weeks are sufficient to destroy any testimony, and the period with which we have to deal was certainly much longer. In face of this uncertainty at the very beginning it may seem vain to expect a solid basis for the Christian tradition. At the best we can only take our stand on a record which was stabilised after the mischief had already been done. For that part, the effort to stabilise was itself a confession that the facts were growing doubtful. Christian teachers were conscious that unless some measure was taken to arrest the process of disintegration the history would soon be lost. Have we any ground for believing that in their attempt to conserve a genuine tradition they were not too late?

It is necessary, at the outset, to protest against the common assumption that little was remembered of Jesus after his death, and that even these scanty memories were preserved by some freak of accident. Our Gospels are themselves the best evidence that this supposition is false. Whatever their value may be, it cannot be denied that they exist, and contain a history which purports to be that of Jesus. They were written in the second generation, but were made from a number of documents which must have been current for something like twenty years. Now it was not these documents which created an interest in the life of Jesus. They were written, it cannot be doubted, to satisfy an interest that was widely felt. From the very outset there seems to have been a general desire to know more about Jesus as he had manifested himself on earth. That he had passed out of memory, even for the world at large, is simply incredible. He had attracted wide attention in his lifetime, and the circumstances of his death had been public and notorious. Paul, addressing Agrippa, can take for granted that the king, as a Jew, is well-informed on the facts, "for this thing was not done in a corner" (Acts 26:26). For some time after his death Jesus must have been the subject of heated discussion in Jewish circles, and much more so when a sect came into being which proclaimed that he was the Messiah and had risen from the dead. All who had come into contact with him, whether they were friendly or hostile, would be eager to report what they knew, as always happens after the death of any man who has made himself conspicuous. Within the church itself he was now revered as the Lord who would presently appear in glory, and whose return might be looked for at any hour. This new attitude to Jesus would not obliterate the thought of his life. It must rather have vastly enhanced its meaning, so that every detail of it was now doubly memorable. Again and again in the Gospels we are told that some action of Jesus was not recalled or understood until after he had risen from the dead; and this notice, we can well believe, reflects the mood of the disciples as they looked back on their fellowship with him. They would examine with new eyes everything he had done, seeking for some deeper significance which they had missed.

Moreover, during all that early period the followers of Jesus were carrying on an ardent mission. They might themselves have been content with the knowledge that whatever he had been on earth he was now the glorified Messiah, but how were they to communicate this faith to others? They were asked continually "who was this Jesus? what did he say or do that will convince us of the claim you make for him?" Unless they had an answer to such questions it is difficult to see that they could have made a single convert. Whether they wished or not, they were compelled to make the life of Jesus the textbook of their message. Missionaries to-day have always to impart the necessary knowledge about Jesus before anything they say is intelligible. It must have been much the same with the earliest missionaries—all the more so because they addressed themselves to Jews, who were already acquainted with all that concerned the Messianic hope. The one thing they demanded was some concrete proof from the life of Jesus that this was indeed the Messiah foretold by the prophets.

It was impossible, then, that the history of Jesus should have fallen into oblivion after his death. The interest in him must have been keener then than in his life-time, and the work of the Christian teacher must have consisted mainly in imparting the information which every one was demanding. According to the book of Acts when the disciples were called on to appoint a colleague, his qualifications were stated by Peter: "Wherefore of those men who have companied with us all the time that the Lord Jesus went in and out among us, beginning from the baptism of John until that same day when he was taken up from among us, must one be ordained to be a witness with us of his resurrection" (Acts. 1:21, 22). It matters little whether Luke here recounts a definite incident. He describes the conditions on which it was known that Christian teachers were appointed in the primitive time. They were the custodians of the tradition, and it was required of them that they should have learned it, as far as possible, at first hand. Luke himself, it may be noted incidentally, claims to stand in the succession of those early teachers. He did not have the personal knowledge of Jesus, but relies on the testimony of those who had. He describes the ministry from the days of John the Baptist onwards, "following the course of all things accurately from the first." His aim is to do in writing what the early witnesses had done by the spoken word.

We are not to think, therefore, of the memory of Jesus surviving by accident, and only in meagre fragments. Everything would seem to indicate that the church maintained its interest in his life, and had many sources of information. It may be surmised, too, that its knowledge did not consist, as is often assumed, in bare notices which were afterwards expanded into narratives. The usual process would be just the opposite one. An Eastern story-teller describes the simplest incident with a wealth of dramatic detail, and his audience is disappointed unless the story is thus amplified. We must conceive of the accounts of Jesus as originally presented with great fulness, and as undergoing a gradual compression at the hands of successive teachers. The central incident of each narrative would be preserved, while it was disencumbered of all the minor circumstances which served no purpose except to make it more realistic. It has often been observed that although Mark is much the shortest Gospel it is the most diffuse. The work of Matthew and Luke is largely one of pruning the exuberance of Mark's narrative, often at the sacrifice of its colour and freshness. In all probability Mark is the fullest in detail because he is the earliest of the evangelists. He stands closest to the primitive narrators, and still possesses something of their manner, although he has doubtless done his best to abridge and compress. The story of the madman of Gadara is a typical instance. Though of minor importance it is told at length with a number of graphic additions which the other two evangelists have discarded as unnecessary. Mark, it may be presumed, has told the story much as it was told in the early days; and all the Gospel narratives, though now confined in many instances to two or three verses, may originally have been drawn out after the same fashion. The effort of the later teachers was to abbreviate—not to expand or embroider what had come to them as fragmentary notes.

So it may be inferred that the chief trouble, at the outset, was the excess of material. All who could tell anything about Jesus were eager to come forward, and much that they offered was of trivial value. Paul may have partly had this in mind when he declared that he did not wish to know Christ after the flesh. He could not but feel that a great deal of the tradition as commonly reported had little or no bearing on the vital interests of the Gospel. It might be interesting in a biographical way, but tended only to obscure the supreme significance of Jesus. Not only would the stories told of him be sometimes trifling and irrelevant, but they would be mixed up with doubtful elements. The narrators would give rein to their imagination. In order to impress their hearers they would distort the facts and add many fanciful touches. That this was done we have evidence in our Gospels—particularly in the accounts of miracles. When once it was recognised that Jesus did things that were extraordinary there was a natural temptation to make them more and more wonderful. All that he did was exaggerated in the telling, and marvels were attributed to him which had sometimes little basis in fact.

In view of this miscellaneous character of the tradition it was necessary that the things of genuine value for Christian faith and living should be singled out and formulated. It was necessary, too, to distinguish between the history and that growing mass of legend which threatened to submerge it. Early in the second century apocryphal Gospels appear to have sprung up everywhere. Many of them were the deliberate invention of heretical teachers, but they doubtless included material which had come down from the previous age. Some of it has found its way into our present Gospels, for instance in the Nativity stories; and if the work of selection had been delayed much longer the whole history of Jesus might have been lost in a morass of fable. This was apparent to those early teachers who made it their task to ascertain and to fix the authentic tradition. Their motive, it cannot be affirmed too strongly, was in the last resort a religious one. The message they proclaimed was bound up with the reality of the life of Jesus. They believed that through him a divine power had come into the world, and before there could be any gospel it was necessary to make sure of the historical facts on which it rested. This was apparent to the writer of Hebrews, who perceives that if Jesus is a true High-Priest he must have lived a human life, he must have suffered and been tempted as we are (Heb. 2:17, 18). It was no less apparent to Paul, who indeed directs his faith to the glorified Lord but centres everything on the conviction that this exalted Lord is one with Jesus, who had lived and died in the manner vouched for by his Apostles. This, from the outset, had been the cardinal Christian belief, and all responsible teachers had a vital interest in the purity of the tradition. Mere legends about Jesus, even if they were intended to magnify him, were useless for the purpose of the message. If the acts attributed to Jesus had not been done by him they could afford no ground for Christian faith. In like manner it was essential that his teaching should be preserved in authoritative form. For his followers it was not merely a lofty ideal ethic but a binding rule of life. He was "the Lord," to whose will they were subject. In the act of baptism they had undertaken to obey him, and must know definitely the nature of his commands.

The need for stabilising the tradition was thus apparent, and a time came when this task was deliberately carried out. Had it been delayed until the harm was done? There was a period, however brief, when the memory of Jesus had been left wholly to common report. Not only so, but it was just in this period that the church was in a fever of apocalyptic excitement, and was prone to accept visions for certainties. Was there any means during those earliest years whereby the record was controlled and safe-guarded? The later teachers, like Paul, delivered what they had received, and this tradition was ever afterwards normative for the church. But what was it that had been received, after rumour and fancy and extravagant hopes had worked their will, during those years of flux at the beginning?

That changes had crept in can hardly be doubted. According to Papias, Mark took his information from Peter, and if this were so we might feel on solid ground, though even Peter's memory after a lapse of years could not be entirely trusted. But the statement of Papias is open to question, and in any case can have reference only to a small part of Mark's material. His Gospel, like the others, does not consist of the reminiscences of any one man, but of the general tradition of the church. The value of the history thus depends on the quality of that tradition, which had certainly become mingled with doubtful elements, or the work of selection would not have been necessary. But there are good grounds for believing that underneath all the accretions and perversions a genuine record maintained itself, which later teachers were able to sift out and formulate. Even in the earliest years, when all was apparently at the mercy of chance, a number of checks were operative, which ensured the preservation of the facts.

(1) The chief of these was the presence in the community of men who had personally known Jesus. His disciples, probably all of them, were about his own age, and would be under forty when he died. At least some of them would survive through the greater part of the first generation. They were for some time the leading teachers of the church, and while they lived were the outstanding figures in that Palestinian community in which the record took shape. We need not suppose that it was submitted to them in every detail for confirmation; but the fact that these men were still alive would act as a restraint. All the narrators would be conscious that their statements might be challenged by those who were in a position to know. The teaching of the disciples was the norm by which all accounts of Jesus had to be controlled, and this is plainly recognised by Paul in his references to what he had received. In his interpretation of the gospel he claims entire freedom, under the guidance of the Spirit, but he acknowledges that on the historical facts there can be no appeal beyond the word of the Apostles.

(2) Again, the record was transmitted in Palestine, under conditions which were much the same as in Jesus' lifetime. Ideas and customs, methods of government, party divisions, had undergone no change. A framework was thus given to which the history had to con-

form, and to this extent a limit was placed on free invention. Every one could see at once when an act was ascribed to Jesus which he could not, under the known conditions, have performed. One has only to think of the later time when the wildest fictions were able to impose themselves, since the world in which Jesus had moved was now buried in the past. The narrator of the first generation, confined within the bounds of what might have happened, was much more likely to describe what *did* happen.

(3) An effective check was provided, as has been already noted, by Jewish opposition. The missionary was aware that if he made any false statement it would quickly be denounced. He knew that if there were awkward facts in the history he was better to admit them, for if they were concealed or disguised his enemies would bring them forward and use them maliciously. We are repeatedly told in the Gospels of criticisms made on Jesus by unbelievers, and there is no reason to doubt that they were indeed made in his lifetime. "Is not this the carpenter?" "He eats with publicans and sinners." "He casts out devils by Beelzebub." "If he was a prophet he would have known that this woman was a sinner." "If thou art the Christ, come down from the Cross." But the prominence given to such criticisms is no doubt due to a consciousness that they were still being made. The message was proclaimed to a public which was well aware how Jesus had actually lived. Left to themselves the Christian teachers might have been tempted to keep many things in the background, but no

choice was given them. Their only safety was to describe the life of Jesus as it had really been, with no attempt to give a false colour to anything. Misrepresentations could best be answered by a plain statement of facts.

(4) The Christian message itself was a factor in guarding the record. Some emphasis must be laid on this, for it is so often taken for granted that the doctrines which had grown up around the Person of Christ must have obscured the history almost from the outset. Jesus had come to be regarded not as a human being but as the Messiah; his life was construed in terms of prophecy and apocalyptic; memories of him were dissolved into theological symbols. To many modern writers it has appeared self-evident that the rise of Christian doctrine was the fatal obstacle to any true knowledge of Jesus. As the object of the church's faith he ceased to have historical reality. His earthly story was either forgotten altogether or was transformed into a myth, similar to those which had gathered around the divinities of Pagan cults.

Now it may fairly be contended that the doctrines in which the church expressed its faith would have just the contrary effect. For one thing—and this cannot be too often repeated—the message was based on the facts, apart from which it had no meaning. Paul has been charged, above all other teachers, with changing the gospel into a theology and replacing the actual Jesus with an imaginary divine being. Yet it is plain to everybody who has grasped even the elements of Paul's teaching that he builds upon the facts. His whole message resolves itself into this—that Christ, who was the power and wisdom of God, manifested himself in a human life and died for men. The historical fact was for Paul the Christian revelation. This was the fundamental principle of all the early teaching. It may be true to say that the church thought of Jesus theologically, but for this very reason it was compelled to know him as he had really been. The theology consisted in the apprehension of the fact.

Apart from this wider consideration we can see that Christian doctrine made for the protection of the historical record. The chief danger from the very outset was in the exercise of mere fancy on the events of the life of Jesus. Even in the Synoptic Gospels we can trace the desire to heighten his miracles, to credit him with exploits like those of the ancient prophets, to make him the hero of tales borrowed from folk-lore. In the course of the Gentile mission Jesus was assimilated to the demigods, and much of the old mythology was transferred to him. The one aim was to make him extraordinary, to endow him with supernatural powers which had no necessary relation to any spiritual ends. But by its conjunction with the Christian message the record was preserved from these encroachments of fable. Foreign elements might enter into it, but they had to be in keeping with its essential character. It could never be forgotten that Jesus was the Messiah, who had come to do God's will, who had gone about doing good, who in word and act had taught the true way of life. The church's conception of Jesus—we may call it theological if we will—did not pervert the tradition but provided a channel in which it could securely flow. When all is said, the message in which the church believed was itself the outcome of what Jesus had achieved by his life. Faith in the message thus gave a touchstone by which all accounts of his life could be tested. When anything was reported of him which could not be reconciled with the message it was at once felt that he could not have done this thing or spoken that word. This is the test which we still apply to those fantastic modern theories which make him out to have been a political agitator, a theosophical mystic, a fanatical dreamer, an ordinary Rabbi. The primitive church applied the same test, and was saved by its knowledge of the message from false and narrow estimates of the life.

Even in the earliest days, therefore, the tradition was in various ways protected. No one had yet thought of fixing it, and there were many possibilities of error; but the essential facts were sufficiently guarded from perversion. At this point, too, it is well to lay stress on one consideration which is too often left entirely out of sight. If the tradition was orally preserved, and remained fluid for a number of years, this was in some ways a positive advantage. It is indeed true that no record is safe until some kind of fixity has been given to it, and this was soon recognised by the church. Nevertheless there is always a danger when any report is fixed prematurely. Most of our errors with regard to the past have been due to this cause, above all others.

Before the facts had time to become fully known, some one wrote them down. He was only half-informed, and possibly had some interest in putting a false account into circulation; but his version stood as the original and therefore the only authentic one, and was implicitly accepted by all succeeding writers. Any attempt to discard or circumvent it was treated as a breach of historical veracity. A great part of what we call "history" is nothing, if we only knew it, but the parrotlike repetition of those primary documents which were indeed written down at the very time but were never true. For the making of a genuine historical record there needs always to be a period when everything is left fluid. Points of detail, such as names, times, measurements, orders given, cannot indeed be fixed too soon. If they are left to the memory they will soon be confused, and much more when they are entrusted to some one else's memory. But when there is question not of some precise matter of fact but of the whole nature and bearing of an event, time must be allowed for all the reports to come in, and for different judgments to express themselves. This was made possible by that initial period in which there was no formal record of the life of Jesus. The church had not yet committed itself to any set version of the events. Various accounts were current; memories were checked against each other; reflection, criticism, imagination came into play, and undoubtedly there was some loss of literal correctness. Our Gospels, it may be, contain no incident of which it may confidently be said that the thing happened exactly as it is now set down. Yet in that intervening time the facts were enabled to clarify themselves and reveal something of their true import. If the earliest reports were mistaken, the church had not stamped them with an official sanction, and they could still be modified in the light of fuller knowledge. A general picture was forming itself, in which all details could find their right place. Thus the period of loose oral tradition is not to be regarded simply as one of unbridled rumour, in which the history of Jesus became so hopelessly entangled with legend that the truth could no longer be recovered. In some respects that initial period was serviceable to the truth. If some record of Jesus had been written down immediately after his death it would have ranked ever afterwards as primary and fundamental, and for that reason would have blocked the way to all real knowledge. It would have given the facts just as they appeared at the moment, before they had made themselves rightly known or had fallen into their due proportions. Those years in which the church was not committed to any set record gave opportunity, one may say, for free discussion, which is always valuable although much of the talk may seem foolish and irrelevant. While the question is still open it is examined by different minds from many points of view, and by this process the true issues are brought to light. So it was necessary that the church should have an interval in which it could freely consider all the accounts that came to it of the life of Jesus, and allow scope to all manner of opinions. All this time when it seemed to be merely wandering it was unconsciously making up its mind. When measures were at last taken to stabilise the record it was found that most of the work was already accomplished. The later teachers had only to formulate the data which had gradually emerged of their own accord.

We are thus to conceive of the tradition adjusting itself through a period in which all kinds of material were mingled together. In its eagerness to learn more about Jesus the church had welcomed information from every quarter. Much of it was of inferior value, and the wheat and tares, as in the parable, had grown up side by side. The difficulty of the church, it must be repeated, lay not in the scantiness but in the embarrassing plenty of its early records. Ridicule has often been thrown on the wild statement of the Fourth Evangelist that if he told all the things known of Jesus the world would not contain the books (John 20:30; 21:25). It is naturally asked why, if he had so much to tell, he has confined himself to a few incidents—the same, for the most part, as those already recounted in the other Gospels. Yet the statement so deliberately made at the emphatic close of his work may reasonably be supposed to have some foundation. If it had been utterly at variance with notorious fact it would have sounded absurd to readers of his own time as it does to us. The simplest explanation is that at the end of the first century there existed a large number of traditions about Jesus. Some of them had grown up out of later fancy and speculation, but for the most part they had come down from earlier days, and were still circulating among the people, although they had been excluded from the record. Out of the abundant material which had accumulated in the primitive age the church had decided on some things which were to be preserved.

This selection was the more natural as the reminiscences of Jesus consisted of a great many episodes, quite separate from each other. It would have been difficult to break up and remodel a coherent narrative; but the question was only one of choosing from a miscellaneous heap of anecdotes and sayings those which had proved themselves best worth keeping. To many people it has appeared strange and not a little suspicious that the life of Jesus should only have been known in this fragmentary fashion. The conclusion has been drawn that some disaster had overtaken the tradition. By accident or design the greater part of what must once have been a complete history has been concealed from our knowledge; the life as a whole has been submerged, and only a few incidents stand out, like patches of island from a lost territory. But we may be certain that there never was a continuous record. Much was remembered about Jesus, but all in the shape of those separate anecdotes. This, if we reflect on it, is the manner in which every man's life is remembered, before it is purposely made the subject of a biography. Most of us have had occasion to realise how difficult it would be to give any consecutive account of the life-story even of an intimate friend. We know his early life only in the vaguest outline; whole years of his later career are hidden from us; we cannot tell what he has been doing even in the few weeks or days since we met him last. It is only in modern times that biography in the proper sense has been made possible, since it requires access to official documents and collections of letters, easy communication with many persons in scattered localities. In former days the life of any man was only known by its few main landmarks, and by means of these a framework was constructed which was filled in with anecdotal material. So it is wrong to infer that the record of Jesus has been lost or mutilated because it has only come to us in brief episodes. That was the manner in which all knowledge of him would naturally be handed down. A great many incidents were remembered, but there was no means of linking them together or filling in the gaps between them. His followers could recall how on this occasion and that he had done or spoken something that impressed them, but they had never attempted to make a detailed study of his career as a whole. So the little anecdotal sections which make up our Gospels are not to be regarded as fragments, broken off from a narrative which was once complete. They represent the story of Jesus as it had always been told. His disciples did not profess to know all about him. They could only speak of journeys they had made with him, of actions which at one time and another they had seen him perform. The result, it must be granted, is a string of disconnected incidents rather than a history; but it is just in this manner that we all remember the friends whom we seem to have known best.

Here we come on a question which has bulked largely in recent discussion, and has given rise to many doubts and misgivings. It is pointed out that the Gospels are nothing but a mosaic of detached pieces which the evangelists themselves have put together, and from this it is argued that nothing can be rightly known of the true course of the history. What the writers had before them was only a confused mass of anecdotes which they have combined by mere guess-work in a purely arbitrary fashion. We know a number of things which Jesus did, but no clue is given us, for the evangelists themselves did not possess it, to the time or circumstances in which he did them. Thus the history of Jesus, in any proper sense of the word, is veiled from us. It is open to any one to break up the Gospel of Mark into its component pieces and by rearranging them to build up an entirely different history from the traditional one. Any other guess as to the true place of a given incident will be as good as Mark's, since he could have no better conception of the story as a whole than we can form ourselves.

Now to some extent it may be admitted that the order of events in our Gospels is artificial. Matthew and Luke, while they follow Mark in their main outline, are constantly at variance with him and with each other in their placing of various incidents. They are evidently aware that Mark had only been guided by his own judgment, and believe that in some instances it had misled him and needed to be corrected. Very often their motive in changing the order seems to be a purely literary one.

They are anxious (and this is especially true of Matthew) to bring together passages which bear on the same theme, or serve in some way to illustrate each other. Mark himself yields at times to this desire, even when he has to do violence to historical sequence. At Cæsarea Philippi, for instance, after Jesus has declared that as the Messiah he must suffer and die, the narrative proceeds: "And when he had called the people unto him with his disciples also, he said to them: Whoever will come after me let him deny himself and take up his cross and follow me" (Mk. 8:34). It must have been obvious to Mark as it is to ourselves that this address to the people was out of place in circumstances where Jesus was alone with his disciples in a foreign country. The passage can have been brought in for no other reason than that it fitted in with the idea that Jesus, as Messiah, had given the example of suffering. So it has to be recognised that the evangelists are often careless of historical order. They make room for incidents in settings where they will be most effective, and sometimes throw several incidents together and insert them at any convenient break in the narrative. The material has come down in the form of many stray anecdotes, and no pretence is made that the position of every detail can be exactly determined.

None the less, the evangelists set themselves to write history, and have been at pains to get all their data, as far as possible, into historical sequence. Luke expressly tells us that one of his main objects is to arrange the record "in order." No doubt he uses this phrase in a general sense, implying that he has sought to make a readable narrative out of the *disjecta membra* of the tradition; but he also wishes us to understand that the narrative agrees broadly with the true succession of events. It is clear that Mark has exercised great care in the ordering of his various episodes. His method has been simply to recount them, one after another, with the loosest of connecting links, and this is apt to create in the reader the sense of a mere jumble. In our earliest notice of Mark's Gospel by Papias he is said to have stated his facts "correctly but without order"; but this is manifestly an error. It cannot be questioned that Mark has placed the events in a more natural and intelligible order than any other evangelist; and he cannot have done so by accident. He must have worked on his material with reflection and insight. It had come to him from a variety of sources but he has sorted out the scattered notices and shaped them into history.

The view is sometimes put forward that what we now accept as the Gospel history is due to nothing else than this ingenuity of Mark. He knew nothing whatever of the true course of the life of Jesus, and was himself solely responsible for that great story which has so fascinated all succeeding times. This is a melancholy conclusion, and also, it may confidently be affirmed, an absurd one. For one thing, most of the episodes themselves indicate their place in the history. The Baptism must have come at the beginning, and the Passion at the end. The Passion must have been preceded by those events which plainly lead up to it, while most of the illustrative anecdotes must belong to the teaching ministry in Galilee. When they are closely examined it is found that most of them, by their intrinsic character, can be assigned to their place in the earlier or the later part of the ministry. It is hardly too much to say that if nothing were known of the course of Jesus' life it could still be reconstructed, with a fair degree of certainty, from the anecdotes which have come to us. If these were all written on separate cards, which were then thrown together and shuffled a dozen times over, an intelligent man would be able to arrange them in something like the order adopted in our Gospels. Although he had no previous knowledge of the life of Jesus he would perceive, from the inner character of these stories, that they ought to stand in that order. It cannot be supposed, however, that our evangelists entered on their task with minds entirely blank. They must already have been well informed on the life of Jesus, or else their undertaking to write an account of it would have been a sheer impertinence. However they may have obtained their knowledge they must have believed that they were specially qualified to deal with this subject: that is the first inference we are entitled to draw from the very existence of any book. For that part, all instructed Christians of the early days would understand, at least in a general way, how the life of Jesus had shaped itself, for it was only on that condition that the separate stories would have any point or meaning. When an anecdote is told you of some famous man it is assumed that you know about him and can fit this particular thing into the framework of your knowledge. When the ancient minstrel recited some exploit of King Arthur or William Wallace or Robin Hood he could take for granted that his audience were familiar with the history. Each adventure might be complete in itself, but it stood out against a background apart from which it was meaningless. In like manner the Christian who listened to the story of the Temptation or the confession at Cæsarea Philippi would require to know something of Jesus' life as a whole. If this knowledge was wanting it would need in every case to be supplied by some brief summary narrative, such as Luke puts into the mouth of Peter when he met with the heathen centurion Cornelius. "That word which was published throughout all Judæa and began from Galilee, after the baptism which John preached; how God anointed Jesus of Nazareth with the Holy Spirit and with power; who went about doing good and healing all who were oppressed by the devil, for God was with him. And we are witnesses of all that he did in the land of the Jews and in Jerusalem; whom they slew and hanged on a tree; him God raised up on the third day and showed him openly" (Acts 10:37–39). A narrative of this kind, as Luke was well aware, formed the necessary prelude to any attempt to explain the meaning of the message of Christ.

It is thus preposterous to hold that while much was reported in detail about the actions of Jesus, nothing was known of the main outline of his life. The theory has been gravely put forward, but it dissolves of its own accord as soon as we try to think of it coherently. The one thing which every Christian, from the very beginning, was bound to know was the general history of Jesus. Paul takes for granted whenever he mentions the name of Jesus that all his readers have at least this knowledge. There might be ignorance on every point of detail but even the humblest convert could tell who Jesus was, and what course his life had followed before it culminated in his death. Without this elementary knowledge no one could become a Christian. The evangelists also pre-suppose this knowledge on the part of their readers, and on the ground of it they build up their record of how the varied incidents had happened. They differ continually, as historians must always do, in their placing of particular facts; but they are agreed on the broad outline. This, it need not be doubted, had been inseparable, at every stage of the transmission, from the church's account of Jesus.

CONCLUSION

THE problem of origins is always an insoluble one. At the end of his search the explorer comes always on many streams that combine to make the river; and each of them issues from springs which are hidden underground. So the course of Gospel tradition cannot be traced back beyond a certain point. We know that before anything was written the church possessed records of Jesus, but how they originated, or what was their earliest character, we shall never know.

Much has been done, however, by modern criticism to push farther back, though not to dispel, the darkness which conceals the primitive tradition. Even in the last few years a number of new and illuminating facts have been established. If they have led at times to negative results this has been due much more to theories read into them than to the facts themselves.

It may be gathered that the account of Jesus was first transmitted orally, and consisted of a great number of separate anecdotes and sayings. This record was preserved in the Christian community, and was associated with the common worship. It was adapted to the needs and circumstances of the brotherhood and was also employed in support of the Christian message—especially of the central belief that Jesus was the Messiah. While it was still in the oral phase it came to be invested with forms, which were more or less conventional. These conclusions are reasonably certain, and it does not follow from any of them or from all of them together that the record is untrustworthy. Each of the factors that entered into the process of transmission would seem, rather, to make for authenticity. Since it belonged to the community the record was saved from the caprice of individual reporters. Since it remained for some time fluid, it was open to the additions and corrections which were rendered necessary by fuller knowledge. Since it was moulded, at a sufficiently early date, according to set patterns, it was made secure. The church had now selected various episodes and sayings which it deemed peculiarly valuable, and fixed them, by this device of form, in the most approved version. It would indeed be idle to maintain that the whole record, as we now have it, is a literal transcript of historical facts. Changes have manifestly come about in the course of transmission; and this may equally be said of any history that has ever been written. But it may fairly be asserted that the process which led up to the making of our Gospels was not one of wilful distortion. Perhaps there could have been no process which was better fitted to sift out and conserve the substantial truth.

The question of the validity of the Gospels is a literary and historical one, and has to be investigated by critical methods. No end can be served by dogmatic statements that since our religion is founded on the Gospels everything contained in them must be accepted as true. Faith cannot be employed in this manner as a guarantee for historical fact. Nevertheless it is not possible to study the Gospels, even from a purely critical point of view, without some regard to their religious purpose. Whatever their origin may have been they were meant to bear witness to the Christian message, and the nature of that message must be borne in mind before we can assess their value as history. In a very real sense the critical problem depends in the last resort on the religious one.

It might seem at first sight as if the truth of Christianity ought to be separated entirely from historical questions. Jesus may not have lived in just the manner described in the Gospels; he may prove to be a figure more or less legendary; but so long as he is recognised by faith as the ideal of the highest life he has religious value for us. Religion has always been a symbolism, and Jesus is our symbol of God; in him we are able to apprehend the fact of God, and to bring it into living relation to our human life. Faith in Christ does not rest on what he may have been historically, but on the embodiment which is given by this character, whether real or imaginary, to our purest conception of the divine. It is therefore argued that the enquiry into his recorded life is a matter of secondary importance, and that no religious interest can be much affected by the results. Men once believed that Christianity itself was in danger if any jot or tittle of the Gospel history was set aside, and for ages a ban was laid on even the most elementary efforts at criticism. We have now learned that our religion is secure although various parts of the record may be considered doubtful. Would anything vital be lost if criticism were to go further, and explain the whole historical tradition as the outgrowth of later piety and imagination? However the story of Jesus may have arisen it is still valid as the symbolic expression of our religion. It is not Jesus himself who is the substance of the Christian faith but that conception of God and His redeeming purpose which is summed up for us in our thought of Jesus.

A view of this kind has often been put forward, and may be regarded as a survival from those philosophies which were dominant in the middle of last century. According to the Hegelian formula, "the rational is the real," and the inner truth of any phenomenon must be sought in the abstract idea which for the moment has expressed itself under forms of space and time. What we call history is nothing but the unfolding of an immanent reason; and this is eminently true of religious history. Jesus is a landmark in the realisation of the divine idea. Everything in his story which was bound up with ephemeral conditions was of the nature of parable and illusion, and must be stripped away before the truth is disclosed. A century ago this reading of the Gospels appeared to make them more profound and significant, but for a long time now there has been a steady reaction against the type of thought which identifies the real with the abstract. We are coming to recognise that an idea does not properly exist until it takes shape as picture or poem or institution or event. The embodiment is no mere husk or shell which needs to be discarded, but is the perfecting of the idea. The actual is the real.

It is this change of attitude, more than anything else, which accounts for that growing interest in the life of Jesus, of which there have been so many evidences in recent years. To some extent it is no doubt due to a natural curiosity as to the true character of that extraordinary life, which has been at last thrown open to free investigation. It is due still more to a new perception of the unique greatness of Jesus. He was formerly viewed from a distance, through a mist of creed and dogma, and there was always a fear that he might shrink to common stature if he could only be looked at more closely. This fear has proved baseless. With the crumbling of those doctrines which were intended to magnify him, Jesus has become yet grander, and stands out in his own right as the most arresting figure in history. Once more, behind the interest in the record there is an urgent practical motive. Amidst the unexampled difficulties of our time men are seeking for some clear direction. They have not found it in any traditional creed, and much less in any of the social or philosophical substitutes. May it not be that Jesus himself possessed the secret which all his interpreters have missed? If we can only reach back to him as he once lived on earth we may discover his way of deliverance.

These motives, however, all spring from the conviction that in religion, as in all else, the truth must be apprehended as something concrete. In every branch of the church to-day there is a retreat from those formal doctrines which were once accepted as the very substance of Christianity. They have lost their hold, not so much because they have grown doubtful, as because they are merely doctrines. If a revelation is to have meaning for us it must be real in the sense that life itself is. A hundred and fifty years ago Lessing declared that a permanent faith cannot be based on contingent facts of history; and this principle appealed to many as self-evident, and seemed to spell the doom of historical Christianity. Yet the modern mind has found itself driven almost to reverse it. Apart from the facts of history there can be no sure basis for faith. Ideas in themselves have no true existence, and remain outside of our life. Before we can lay hold of God he must enter into this world of reality of which we form a part. The Word must become flesh.

This is the conviction which has always lain at the heart of Christianity, and to which it owes its distinctive character. It is an historical religion, not merely in the sense that we know the date and circumstances of its origin, but in the deeper sense that the history was itself the revelation. God was made known through things that actually happened. "What we have heard, what we have seen with our eyes and have looked upon, and our hands have handled of the word of life, declare we unto you" (I John 1:1). This has always been the essential Christian message, and can be discerned even in types of belief which we rightly condemn as unspiritual. Our sympathy is with the reformers who protested against the image-worship of the Byzantine church and the mediæval cult of sacraments. Yet it needs to be recognised that in those superstitions a genuine religious instinct was at work. The revelation had been given in visible events, and the Christian mind insisted, in however crude a fashion, on that actuality which was inherent in Christian faith. It is this same instinct which is forcing us back, in our own day, to the historical life of Jesus. One cannot but feel, at times, that attention is too much concentrated on the history. Men are in danger of repeating the error of which Paul was afraid when he determined that he would no more know Christ after the flesh. Yet the desire to see Jesus as a definite figure in history is a legitimate and a profoundly Christian one. Our religion was given in a life that was once lived among us, and if we are to recover the religion in its true significance and power, we must begin with a fuller understanding of the life.

The question at issue in the investigation of the Gospels is thus of fundamental import. Is this account of Jesus historical, or must we seek its origin in the pious fancy of the church? Nothing is gained by contending that in either case the record inspires and uplifts us: for there is a world of difference between something imagined and something that has been realised. The loftiest ideal, so long as it is nothing more, can do little to help us. Most often it leaves us with a sense of futility, as we compare that which is with the perfect thing which can never be. Plato, himself a great poet, required that all poets should be banished from his Republic. He was aware that poetry tends only to weaken the nerve of action. From their sojourn among the clouds men turn with distaste and weariness to the work that lies to their hands. And if Christianity is to quicken and direct the lives of men, it must rest on the assurance that the story of Jesus is real. If it could be proved to be nothing more than a glorious legend, woven out of the dreams and longings of the early believers, our religion would fall to the ground. It would cease to have any relation to this world of actuality in which we live. It would be paralysed at the very centre of its power.

This was fully apparent to the Christians of the first century. For them, too, the worth of Jesus' message was bound up with the reality of his life and death; and the first great controversy in the church turned on this very question. According to the so-called Docetic teaching the life of Jesus was only an appearance, since it was inconceivable that the divine nature should ally itself with material existence. Jesus had indeed come to earth and had brought the knowledge of God, but he had only worn the semblance of a human body; he had *seemed* to identify himself with man's common lot, while remaining aloof from it. The Docetists did not question the validity of the Gospel record, but in their own strange manner they reached the same position as that which is often maintained to-day, in the name of the latest criticism. They held that the life of Jesus, while it had a unique spiritual value, was historically unreal. Against this Docetic view all the later New Testament writings are in one way or another directed. The church perceived that by denying reality to the earthly life the heretics had cancelled the whole meaning of the Christian revelation. If Christ had not fully shared the life of men he had effected nothing, for the divine power he was supposed to impart had never entered the world at all. It was the Docetic heresy which compelled the church to state this conviction in explicit terms, but from the outset all Christian thinking was rooted in the belief that the life of Jesus was real. He had appeared in the flesh; he had taught and done and suffered certain things which were fully attested. All teachers were left free to interpret the facts, by the light of scripture and the Spirit; but there must be no dubiety as to the facts themselves.

Most probably we owe our Gospels to nothing else than to this consciousness on the part of the church that fact and interpretation must be kept separate. There was a place for doctrine and mystical vision, but these could have no meaning unless the historical facts were definitely put on record. However the revelation might be understood, it was contained in the life of Jesus as it had once been lived on earth, and the knowledge of this life was the one thing necessary. When Paul contrasts the Jew listening to the law of Moses with the Christian beholding the face of Christ (II Cor. 3:15–18), he may have meant the comparison literally. The worship of the synagogue centred on the reading of the law; that of the church on the recounting of the Gospel narrative. Believers could feel, as they heard the story of Jesus, that he lived again before their eyes; and in this beholding of him the message consisted. Christianity was nothing else than the apprehension of God through the word and action of Jesus.

Here, then, we have the ultimate ground for confidence that in our Gospels we have a genuine historical record. They were written for a religious purpose which they could only fulfil by a true narration of the facts. It is often maintained that in reading the Gospels we must exercise two kinds of judgment, which need to be kept distinct. On the one hand, we must be alive to their religious message; on the other hand, we must examine them critically. In so far as they purport to be works of history they are subject to the ordinary laws of historical evidence, and our conclusions must rest on no other ground. Now it is indeed true that the criticism of the Gospels ought not to be influenced by any religious pre-possessions, but one thing has always to be borne in mind. The religious value of the Gospels cannot be separated from their historical value. It was the Christian belief that God had revealed himself and had wrought salvation through a human life, which was lived in a particular manner, in a given place and time. The religion was contained in the facts which the writings profess to record, and historical fidelity was essential to their religious purpose. The reporters were fully aware that by perverting the record they would destroy its significance. These events had value for Christian faith because they had really happened, and no invention, however impressive, could take the place of the fact. It may be taken as certain that the chief interest of the early teachers, from the oral period onward, was to preserve the truth of the record. Their motive was a religious one. The Christian message, as they understood it, was given in the historical facts, which must therefore be reported just as they were. When Paul recounts the Lord's appearances as he knew them from the Apostles, he declares that if the facts are wrongly stated "we shall be found false witnesses of God" (I Cor. 15: 15). This was the attitude of all teachers who dealt with the Gospel history. They were entrusted with the knowledge of those facts through which God had made his revelation, and were pledged to offer true witness.

The Christian message, it cannot be too often repeated, was the announcement of a fact, and from this point of view the tradition must be understood. To be sure there was a theology, which bulks so largely in the New Testament that it might seem to constitute the whole religion. We conceive of the primitive believers as pre-occupied with certain doctrines which gave rise to a church, and to the story of a half-mythical Lord who had been its founder. But these doctrines were not the distinctive element in early Christianity. There was little in them that was peculiarly new. For almost all of them it is not difficult to find analogies in Judaism, or in the religion and philosophy of the Hellenistic world. Much labour has been expended in tracing out these analogies, and in thus demonstrating that there was nothing original in the message proclaimed by the church. But it was never claimed that the theological ideas were new. They were taken over, more or less consciously, from the thought of the time in order to explain and illustrate the essential message, which consisted simply in the announcement of what Jesus had done. The doctrines were borrowed, but the church added to them one tremendous thing which was absolutely new. It affirmed that what had been desired and hoped for had now become fact. The prophets had foretold a Messiah; he had now come. They had sought to believe that God was merciful and would save his people; Jesus had manifested this divine goodness in action. By a life which men had witnessed with their own eyes all the promises had received the yea and amen. This, as the early church understood it, was the Gospel. Jews and Pagans could argue, as we know they did, that the Christian teachers had nothing to say which they had not heard already, in more impressive language, from their own prophets and mystics and philosophers. But there was one thing which they now heard for the first time. What had hitherto been dream and premonition had been realised, and the Christian teaching was concerned with this reality. Unless it transmitted faithfully the facts of the life of Jesus the church had no message, and no right to exist.

The origin of the Gospels must thus be sought in the very nature of the new religion. If God had revealed himself in events of history a record was necessary, and it must be in strict accordance with the facts. Nothing but a true report could answer the purpose, since the thing that happened was the revelation. It was thus the Christian religion which preserved the record, and which also guided the process by which it was sifted and consolidated. For the Gospels as we have them cannot have been made out of chance reminiscences which had somehow survived after the real history of Jesus had been forgotten. They contain the final result of a long selection, in which the church had fastened, with a sure instinct, on those memories of Jesus which were most characteristic of his life and thought. The proof of this may be found in the sheer excellence of the Gospels. There are no books in the world which bring together within so brief a compass so much that is great and beautiful, and this cannot be due to any accident. An intelligent reader some ages hence who should come on a copy of the *Golden Treasury*, with no clue whatever to its nature, would yet see for himself that it was no mere scrapbook of stray verse. He would perceive, as he read it, that it must have had behind it a great literature, of which it preserved the very quintessence. Must we not arrive at a similar conclusion regarding our Gospels? Out of a rich material the church has given us the best. In some measure, no doubt, it was guided in its choice by its own immediate needs; but it is absurd to think of the early community as concerned wholly with matters of cult and administration. The grand interest of that first community, as of all Christian churches since, was in the religion of Jesus. It chose out those sayings in which he gave utterance to his deepest mind, those incidents in which he stood out most manifestly as the revelation of God's mercy and forgiveness. This response to the message of Jesus was the ultimate factor in the shaping of the records.

Jesus in his own Person is the substance of Christianity, and it is only through the Gospels that we know him as he lived on earth. How far can we trust these narratives, on which our religion, in the final issue, depends? In former times they were fenced around by church doctrine and authority, and were thus guarded against all assault; but this is no longer possible, nor is it consistent with the nature of the Gospels themselves. They claim to record a history, and thereby challenge the same scrutiny as that which is applied to other historical documents. If Christianity were nothing but a mysticism or a philosophy, the religious judgment would be enough; but it bases itself on facts, and we have the right to demand that it should prove the facts. They cannot be proved except by the ordinary methods of historical criticism. Yet all Christian men feel it to be intolerable that their religion should lie at the mercy of academical critics, who will always differ from one another, and whose conclusions are doubtful and fluctuating at the best. Is there no stable ground on which our confidence in the Gospel history may be rested? There is one such ground, which cannot be much affected by any changes of critical opinion. For our knowledge of Jesus we must indeed depend on the records, left to us by those primitive teachers who alone had acquaintance with the facts. Yet we can be certain that they witnessed truly, for their religion was one with the history. They believed that God had revealed himself through Jesus Christ, and for that belief they willingly died. But the revelation had no meaning for them apart from the actual life. They recorded the life with the full consciousness that if Jesus had not lived in this manner their faith was vain. It was in the facts that God had spoken, and by the knowledge of them men would apprehend God. This is our ultimate security for the Gospel record. It is attested by the faith which inspired the early disciples, and through them is living to this day. It can be said of the records, as of the message which they proclaim: "therein is the righteousness of God revealed, from faith to faith."

BIBLIOGRAPHY

BIBLIOGRAPHY

THE enquiry into the validity of the Gospels involves a
multitude of questions, critical, historical and theological. No
complete account of the literature is possible, but the following list of books will at least indicate some of the relevant
lines of study. The books selected are not in every case the
best, but they are easily accessible, and are typical of the modern investigation in its more important aspects.

LIVES OF JESUS

Bousset, Wilhelm, *Jesus* (English translation).

Case, S. J., *Jesus, a New Biography.*

Eisler, Robert, *Messiah-Jesus.* (English translation.) A monu-
ment of vast misdirected learning.

Goguel, M., *Vie de Jésus.* (English translation.) Perhaps the
fullest and most judicious of the more recent "Lives."

Guignebert, C. A. H., *Jésus.* (English translation.) A work
of great ability, written from an unduly negative point
of view.

Headlam, A. C., *Life and Teaching of Jesus, the Christ.*

Klausner, J., *Jesus of Nazareth.* (Translated from Hebrew.)
By an eminent Jewish scholar, with a strong Jewish
bias; but for that reason peculiarly interesting and valuable.

Merejkowski, D. S., *Jesus the Unknown.* (English translation.)

—— *Jesus Manifest.* (English translation.) Two wildly
erratic books, with flashes of deep insight, only possible
to a man of genius.

Schweitzer, Albert, *Quest of the Historical Jesus.* (English
translation.)

Warschauer, Joseph, *The Historical Jesus*.
Wernle, D. P., *Jesus*. (English translation.)

THE SYNOPTIC PROBLEM

Buckley, E. R., *Introduction to the Synoptic Problem*.
Burkitt, F. C., *The Gospel History and Its Transmission*.
Cadbury, H. J., *The Making of Luke—Acts*.
Goodspeed, E. J., *An Introduction to the New Testament*.
Lake, Kirsopp and Silva, *An Introduction to the New Testament*.
Moffatt, James, *Introduction to the New Testament*.
Stanton, V. H., *The Gospels as Historical Documents*.
Streeter, B. H., *The Four Gospels*.
Taylor, V., *The Synoptic Problem*.

FORM CRITICISM

Bultmann, R., *Die Geschichte der synoptischen Evangelien*.
Dibelius, M., *From Tradition to Gospel*. (English translation.)
Easton, B. S., *The Gospel before the Gospels*.
Fascher, E., *Formgeschichte*.
Grant, F. C., *Form Criticism*. (A translation of short books by D. Rudolf Bultmann and Karl Kundsin.)
Schmidt, K. L., *Der Rahmen der Geschichte Jesu*.

THE PRIMITIVE CHURCH

Dobschütz, Ernst, *Christian Life in the Primitive Church*. (English translation.)
Lietzmann, Hans, *The Beginnings of the Christian Church*.
—— *The Founding of the Church Universal*. (Translation of the first two volumes of *Die Geschichte der Alten Kirche*.
Linton, O., *Das Problem der Urkirche*.
Lowrie, W., *The Church and Its Organisation*.

Macdonald, A. B., *Christian Worship in the Primitive Church.*

McGiffert, A. C., *The Apostolic Age.*

Pfleiderer, Otto, *Primitive Christianity.* (English translation.)
This work and McGiffert's, though written in the last
generation, are still of first-rate value.

Ropes, J. H., *The Apostolic Age in the Light of Modern
Criticism.*

Streeter, B. H., *The Primitive Church.*

Weiss, Johannes, *Das Urchristentum.*

Weizsacker, K. H., *The Apostolic Age of the Christian
Church.* (English translation.)

THE JEWISH TRADITION

Abrahams, Israel, *Studies in Pharisaism and the Gospels.* 1st
and 2nd Series.

Box, G. H., *The Religion and Worship of the Synagogue.*

Finkelstein, Louis, *Akiba.*

Herford, R. T., *Pharisaism, Its Aim and Its Method.*

—— *Christianity in Talmud and Midrash.*

Montefiore, C. J., *Rabbinic Literature and Gospel Teachings.*

Moore, G. F., *Judaism.* 3 vols.

Oesterley, W. O. E., *Judaism and Christianity.* Vol. I.

Strack, H. C.—Billerbeck, Paul, *Kommentar zum Neuen
Testament.* 4 vols. An indispensable store-house of Rabbinical parallels.

PAUL AND THE LIFE OF JESUS

Feine, K. E. P., *Neutestamentliche Theologie.*

Goguel, Maurice, *L'Apôtre Paul et Jésus Christ.*

—— *Jesus the Nazarene.* (English translation.)

Holtzmann, H. J., *Neutestamentliche Theologie.*

Meyer, Eduard, *Ursprung und Anfänge des Christentums.*

Morgan, W., *Religion and Theology of Paul.*

Porter, F. C., *The Mind of Christ in Paul.*

Weinel, Heinrich, *Neutestamentliche Theologie.*

TEACHING OF JESUS

Bacon, B. W., *Studies in Matthew*.
Branscomb, B. H., *Jesus and the Law of Moses*.
—— *The Teachings of Jesus*.
Dalman, G. F., *Die Worte Jesu*.
Dodd, C. H., *The Parables of the Kingdom*.
Jülicher, Adolf, *Die Gleichnisreden Jesu*.
Manson, T., *The Teaching of Jesus*.
Smith, B. M. T., *The Parables of the Synoptic Gospels*.
Wrede, W., *Die Worte Jesu*.

COMMENTARIES ON THE GOSPELS

Easton, B. S., *St. Luke*.
Loisy, A. F., *Les évangiles synoptiques*.
McNeile, A. H., *The Gospel According to St. Matthew*.
James Moffatt New Testament Commentary, the vols. on
    Matthew, Mark and Luke.
Montefiore, C. G., *The Synoptic Gospels*. (Revised edition.)
Rawlinson, A. E. J., *St. Mark*.
Weiss, J., *Die Schriften des Neuen Testaments*. Vol. I.

GENERAL

Burkitt, F. C., *Christian Beginnings*.
Dodd, C. H., *The Apostolic Preaching*.
Jackson, F. J. Foakes, and Lake, K., *Beginnings of Christianity*.
    Vols. I and II.
James, M. R., *The Apocryphal Gospels*.
Lightfoot, R. H., *History and Interpretation in the Gospels*.
McGiffert, A. C., *Christianity as History and Faith*.
Morgan, W., *The Nature and Right of Religion*.
Norden, Edward, *Agnostos Theos*.

INDEX

INDEX

Abundance of early material,
148, 164f., 179
Acts, book of, 35, 60, 64, 166
Actuality, 191, 195
Agabus, 69
Agrippa, 165
Albertz, M., 83, 133
Alexandrian theology, 50
Anthologies, 149
Antioch, 59, 111
Apocalyptic, 171
Apocrypha, 2, 169
Apollos, 80
Apostles' Creed, 36
Apostolic preaching, 68
Arabian tales, 140
Aramaic, 59, 114, 117, 138

Beatitudes, 125
Biography, modern, 181
Boswell, 126
Bousset, W., 85
Branscomb, B. H., 4
Brotherly love, 65
Bultmann, D. R., 133
Bunyan, 17
Byzantine church, 193

Cæsar, 39, 137
Cæsarea Philippi, 183
Case, S. J., 54
Checks on tradition, 172f.
Christian community, 9, 54, 85ff.
Church meeting, 66f.
Church practice, 10
Claudius, 17

Controversy, 50, 83f.
Corinth, 68
Cornelius, 186
Couchod, 16, 69
Council of Jerusalem, 110
Cromwell, 23

Defoe, 140
Dibelius, M., 65, 68, 111, 117,
133, 135
Divorce, 55, 84
Docetism, 195
Doctrine, 174f., 192
Dodd, C. H., 27
Doublets in Gospels, 13
Drews, 16

Eastern story-telling, 167
Easton, B. S., 133, 134
Elders, testimony of, 160
Enthusiasm in worship, 70
Esquimaux, 77
Eusebius, 160
Example of Christ, 153

Fact as revelation, 175
Faith in Christ, 41, 137, 190
Fascher, E., 133
Fixity of record, 163
Forgiveness, 53
Form, meaning of, 134ff.
Formgeschichte, 39, 115f.
Formulation, process of, 129, 144
Fourth Gospel, 48f., 179, 202

Gadara, madman of, 168

211